# GOVERNANCE OF THE EXTENDED ENTERPRISE

# GOVERNANCE OF THE EXTENDED ENTERPRISE

## Bridging Business and IT Strategies

*IT Governance Institute*

**WILEY**

John Wiley & Sons

**Disclaimer**
The IT Governance Institute (ITGI), Information Systems Audit and Control
Association and the authors of *Governance of the Extended Enterprise* have designed
the publication primarily as an educational resource for control professionals. ITGI,
ISACA, and the authors make no claim that use of this product will assure a successful
outcome. The publication should not be considered inclusive of any proper procedures
and tests or exclusive of other procedures and tests that are reasonably directed to
obtaining the same results. In determining the propriety of any specific procedure
or test, the controls professional should apply his/her own professional judgment to
the specific control circumstances presented by the particular systems or information
technology environment.

*Library of Congress Cataloging-in-Publication Data:*

ISBN: 0-471-33443-X

Printed in the United States of America

10 9 8 7 6 5 4 3 2 1

# About the Author

## IT Governance Institute®

The IT Governance Institute (ITGI) (*www.itgi.org*) was established in 1998 to advance international thinking and standards in directing and controlling an enterprise's information technology. Effective IT governance helps ensure that IT supports business goals, optimizes business investment in IT, and appropriately manages IT-related risks and opportunities. The IT Governance Institute offers symposia, original research, and case studies to assist enterprise leaders and boards of directors in their IT governance responsibilities.

## Information Systems Audit and Control Association®

With more than 35,000 members in more than 100 countries, the Information Systems Audit and Control Association (ISACA®) (*www. isaca.org*) is a recognized worldwide leader in IT governance, control, security, and assurance. Founded in 1969, ISACA sponsors international conferences, publishes the *Information Systems Control Journal™*, develops international information systems auditing and control standards, and administers the globally respected Certified Information Systems Auditor™ (CISA®) designation, earned by more than 35,000 professionals since inception, and the Certified Information Security Manager™ (CISM™) designation, a groundbreaking credential earned by 5,000 professionals in its first two years.

# Contents

# Acknowledgments

IT Governance Institute wishes to recognize:

- The Ministry of International Trade and Industry, Japan, for its sponsorship of the project.
- The Board of Trustees, for its support of the project:

    *Marios Damianides,* CISA, CISM, CA, CPA, Ernst & Young LLP, United States, International President

    *Abdul Hamid Bin Abdullah,* CISA, CPA, FIIA, Auditor General's Office, Singapore, Vice President

    *William C. Boni,* CISM, Motorola, United States, Vice President

    *Ricardo Bria,* CISA, SAFE Consulting Group, Spain, Vice President

    *Everett C. Johnson,* CPA, Deloitte & Touche LLP, United States, Vice President

    *Howard Nicholson,* CISA Mortgage Choice, Australia, Vice President

    *Bent Poulsen,* CISA, CISM, VP Securities Services, Denmark, Vice President

    *Frank Yam,* CISA, CIA, CCP, CFE, Focus Strategic Group Inc., Hong Kong, Vice President

    *Robert S. Roussey,* CPA, University of Southern California, United States, Past International President

    *Paul A. Williams,* FCA, Paul Williams Consulting, United Kingdom, Past International President

    *Emil D'Angelo,* CISA, CISM, Bank of Tokyo-Mitsubishi, United States, Trustee

*Ronald Saull,* CSP, Great-West Life and IGM Financial, Canada, Trustee

*Erik Guldentops,* CISA, CISM, Belgium, Advisor, IT Governance Institute

- The GIEE project committee:

    *Akira Matsuo,* CISA, CPA, ChoAoyama Audit Corp., Japan, Chair

    *Lily M. Shue,* CISA, CISM, CCP, CITC, LMS Associates LLC, United States, Chair

    *Kiyoshi Endo,* CISA, ChoAoyama Audit Corporation, Japan

    *John W. Lainhart IV,* CISA, CISM, IBM, United States

    *Hugh A. Parkes,* CISA, FCA, Stanton Consulting Partners, Australia

    *Deepak Sarup,* CISA, FCA, Siam Commercial Bank, Thailand Singapore

    *Patrick Stachtchenko,* CISA, CA, Deloitte & Touche Solutions, France

    *Hitoshi Takase,* SAP, Japan

    *Thomas C. Lamm,* Information Systems Audit and Control Association, United States

    *Linda S. Wogelius,* Information Systems Audit and Control Association, United States

The authors wish to acknowledge the contributions of:

    *Susan Caldwell,* Information Systems Audit and Control Association, United States

    *Tomoyasu Eto,* CISA, Computer Engineering & Consulting, Japan

    *Erik Guldentops,* CISA, CISM, Belgium

    *Nobuko Kogori,* INES, Japan

    *Lynn C. Lawton,* CISA, BA, FCA, FIIA, PIIA, KMPG, United Kingdom

    *J. Kristopher Lonborg,* Ernst & Young, United States

    *Toru Maki,* INES, Japan

    *Shuji Miyazawa,* ITEC, Japan

    *Robert G. Parker,* CISA, CA, FCA, CMC, Deloitte & Touche, Canada

    *Tsutomu Suzuki,* Cambridge Technology Partners, Japan

*Ira R. Weiss,* Ph.D., Dean, Northeastern University, United States

*Paul A. Williams,* FCA, MBCS, Paul Williams Consulting, United Kingdom

## Expert Reviewers

*Michael P. Cangemi,* CISA, CPA, *IS Control Journal,* United States

*Jean-Pierre Corniou,* Renault Group, France

*Dean R.E. Kingsley,* CISA, CISM, CA, Deloittte Touche Tohmatsu, Australia

*Chitoshi Koga,* Ph.D., Kobe University, Japan

*Jan LaHayne,* CIO, Littelfuse, United States

*Eiichi Matsubara,* Gartner, Japan

*Robert McLaughlin,* Sony Electronics, Inc., United States

*Thomas L. Putalik,* PE, Improved Performance Technologies, United States

*Robert S. Roussey,* CPA, Leventhal School of Accounting, University of Southern California, United States

*Ronald Saull,* CSP, Great-West Life and IGM Financial, Canada

# Preface

The phenomenon, where an organization extends outside its traditional boundaries, is commonly described as an *extended enterprise*, a *virtual enterprise*, or even a *virtually integrated enterprise*. As the diversity of the e-business environment proliferates, the real benefits for an organization will be attained by those entities that endorse and embrace this extended enterprise concept and adapt to best fit the environment in which they operate. In an extended enterprise, the core focus replaces a centralized one, and there is a shift to shared services, cosourcing and outsourcing, extending out to partners, suppliers, and customers to accomplish the objectives more effectively.

This book is designed to detail the main concepts of governance, how the issue transcends beyond the physical boundaries of an enterprise, how it has extended out into entities' customers, trading partners and suppliers, and the interdependencies that have been created. It provides new ideas and ways to think, utilizing concepts that are familiar and accepted by business and governmental entities. Although the topic of governance may be a familiar concept, applying that outside of the physical walls of an organization, and in tandem with a partner, supplier, or customer, is a relatively new concept, and certainly one that is not well accepted yet in the marketplace. However, the advent of the Internet, and the technologies related to it, has created the opportunity and the need to seize the advantages of operating in the extended enterprise. Globalization and worldwide communications have overridden traditional boundaries. In many markets, these global interdependencies (governmental, political, and business) are now so interconnected that they must be considered with almost any decision being made. Additionally, information technology (IT) has moved from being an enabler of organization strategy to a key element of it. The governance of IT can no longer be easily separated from overall enterprise governance. It is uncertain how well the current governance frameworks, developed to serve the post-industrial society, can be adapted to serve the needs of the globally extended information- and knowledge-based enterprises of today.

Therefore, it is time to consider other ways of dealing with this changed environment.

The text will assist readers in becoming familiar with the critical issues of concern related to doing business, and doing it with world-class excellence in this new environment called the extended enterprise. It has often been stated that information is the grease that allows an enterprise to run efficiently. This statement, when related to extended enterprises, can mean the difference between success and failure, and profit or loss. A few examples of what can happen when an effective governance approach is not in place to deal with those issues that reside outside of the physical walls of the extended environment are as follows:

- Cisco Systems wrote off $2.5 billion in inventory, due to poor information and management of co-sourced partners and suppliers.
- Micron Technologies wrote down $260 million of memory, or 32 percent of revenue, due to problems in the value chain.
- IBM lost 16 percent of its value in one day because of various component shortages due to lack of adequate partner and supplier communication and information.

The intent of this book is to be useful for the executive responsible and concerned with governance. It offers useful advice to those with process ownership responsibility, as well as to users of those processes. Although the book explores the issue of responsibility for governance, it does so primarily from several angles: first from the inside looking inside, then from the inside looking outside, and finally from the outside looking inside. The text presents a philosophy for looking at the governance of an entity in a traditional centralized approach, as well as the more nimble and flexible manner using the core as the focus.

This book is also intended for the risk manager, control and assurance professional. Security and business architecture managers will find many ideas not only for their review responsibilities, but to add value as a consultant to the process owner. Although this book was primarily written for the decision maker in both business and governmental entities, it will also be of great use to those focusing in specific specializations within those enterprises.

An international team of professionals has developed a process for change and a governance model for an extended enterprise, as described in this book. In developing this process and model, the latest emerging practices from major information and knowledge businesses have been considered and included. As such, it represents a major new knowledge resource for enterprises, as well as opening up new avenues of practice in strategy setting, enterprise management, control assessment, risk management and in providing assurance. The ultimate aim is to provide a benchmark against which current enterprise practices can be compared and, as a corollary, improved upon. As such, the book contains a number of suggested maturity models that can be used and tailored. The book includes such topics as:

- Vision/leadership
- Strategy development with value innovation
- Performance management to ensure value creation
- Operational business activities which lead to the realization of value/ benefit
- Understanding of a governance structure, its criteria, and a suggested framework
- Enterprise architecture, its importance to the business, and showing how to implement an appropriate governance structure
- Questions of importance for boards and senior management related to these issues

# INTRODUCTION

The boundaries of today's organizations are more flexible and dynamic and, in most cases, more extensive. Organizations and industries realize that they must start focusing on whole processes, including those that transcend the physical walls of the entity. They must reach out to business partners, suppliers, and customers. Such organizational structure is often referred to as the *extended enterprise*. "Modern structures—in business, in society, in politics—must be open and flexible if they are to keep up with the pace of change. To use a military analogy, old corporate structures resembled those of cold war armies—massive, centralized, and focused on a well-defined enemy. New structures must be more like rapid deployment forces, able to go wherever needed and to get there fast."[1] Enterprises today are trying to define exactly the role required of partners and outside vendors. The U.S. Sarbanes-Oxley Act and the recent EU Directive are causing a large shift in thinking.

Although an organization's view of its trading partners may remain unchanged, the interaction with them has dramatically increased. Entities are leveraging each other's expertise and specialties in support of an end-to-end process. "The new economy has three distinguishing characteristics: it is global; it favors intangible things—ideas, information, and relationships; and it is intensely interlinked. These three attributes produce a new type of market place and society, one that is rooted in ubiquitous electronic networks."[2]

Accurate, appropriate, and timely information is the indispensable component in the new economy or, commonly referred to as, the extended enterprise. Information/knowledge-sharing activity among stakeholders of the extended enterprise is a key success factor in delivering workable enterprise governance. To use knowledge effectively, knowledge must be leveraged to drive business value, learning and organizational change.

An overall competitive strategy must drive an effective knowledge management strategy and leadership. To achieve this, an organization must:

- Build an appropriate information organization to provide the information required by senior management in decision making.
- Build an IT leadership team that will understand the business goals and objectives, so that IT can be harnessed to support those goals and objectives.
- Stay current with the technologies that support the business architecture and needs.
- Institute a business process to manage information technology change.
- Improve the organization's ability to perform its mission and indirectly increase the information team's effectiveness and credibility.

Michael Hammer, one of the world's leading authors on business strategy, stated that as global competition grows, organizations are turning to virtual integration, which lets them concentrate solely on the processes in which they know they can be world-class and have a competitive advantage. They will then rely on, or partner with, someone outside the entity to perform the rest.[3] This phenomenon of extending an organization outside its traditional boundaries is commonly described as *extended enterprise, virtual enterprise,* or *virtual integration enterprise.* As the diversity of the commerce environment proliferates, the real benefits of the extended enterprise will be attained by those entities that endorse and embrace this concept.

## MANAGING CHANGE AS A BUSINESS PROCESS

To achieve success in organizing a business process to manage change, people must change their behavior to sustain the change and manage the change systematically as a business process. As stated by Therese Morin, "To effectively manage change as a business process, one must consider creating a change vision, developing change leadership, communicating the change vision and building commitment, configuring the change program, managing the change program and sustaining the change."[4]

"The accelerating pace of business change exposes the weakness of existing business structures, diminishing your company's ability to capture new opportunities or respond to new challenge. It will be increasingly important to develop two core capabilities, beyond what is in place today:

- The ability to manage an organization's culture for change

- The ability to build on an enterprise technology architecture that will support seizing new business opportunities rapidly . . ."[5]

There are multiple forces that are changing today's business environment. Some of those forces include doing business with no boundaries, where the product life cycle has been reduced and competition, buyer information, and expectation have increased. To meet this challenge, the organization must have the ability to reinvent itself and to build and execute a new business architecture and model.

## HOW DO WE GET THERE FROM HERE?

There are various ways to reach the new business architecture and model. The change would include a new enterprise architecture, a new framework, and a new enterprise hierarchy of business dynamics.

This guideline suggests the provision of a core repository of information—referred to as a *knowledge-portal knowledge base* for the extended enterprise. The core repository of information specifically focuses on:

- Vision/leadership
- Value creation and performance management
- Governance framework and criteria
- Governance officer
- Enterprise architecture implementation

## VISION/LEADERSHIP

Organizations should seek to distribute power and function to the maximum degree and seek infinite durability, malleability, and diversity. Transformation must involve the entire organization, with top management leading the effort. Only a new and shared perception of the entity's opportunities can lead to new ways to compete. Managers must have a clear understanding of the elements of the transformation efforts. If they cannot see and understand the future, they cannot create value or innovation, let alone accept and own the transformation process. Chapters 1 and 2 of the text deal with these concepts, drivers of change, and lay out some suggested solutions for dealing with issues that might be experienced by those enterprises, business as well as governmental, looking to conduct business within the extended enterprise.

## VALUE CREATION AND PERFORMANCE MANAGEMENT

Business units and information leaders are now required to measure performance objectives in terms of results achieved, rather than in terms of resources and efforts expended. Implementing a performance measurement tool, such as the *business balanced scorecard,* with an extended enterprisewide information system equipped by a knowledge portal could be a new strong internal control system that is able to replace the traditional internal control system. Monitoring is a fundamental piece of the extended enterprise governance model. Part of management's stewardship responsibility is to make certain that what was agreed to be done is being done and to be constantly evaluating to determine if it will need to be done in the future.

Good governance should provide proper incentives for each of the stakeholders to pursue. The objectives that are pursued need to be in the best interests of the organization and its stakeholders, and facilitate effective monitoring thereby encouraging stakeholders to use resources more efficiently.

The IT Governance Institute provides a straightforward architecture for the performance measurement process. Objectives, goals and expectations of an enterprise are set (plan and organize):

- Means of attaining those objectives through enterprise activities and utilization of the enterprise's resources are determined (acquire, implement, deliver, and support)
- Monitoring and reporting performance guidelines are established and controlled (monitor and evaluate)
- Organizational structure and accountabilities are implemented for effective governance

Chapters 3 and 4 of the text address the topics of value creation and strategy implications, and various methods of performance measurement and monitoring. Finally, operational business issues are described and a blueprint for sharing and communicating in the extended enterprise is presented.

## GOVERNANCE FRAMEWORK AND CRITERIA

The business world today is gripped by tremendous crosscurrents concerning the philosophy and practice of governance. Many traditional industrial entities had concentrated power in executive management. However, recently some of the most successful organizations have implemented radical changes in their governance systems. In part, this has been attributed to the passing of the Sarbanes-Oxley Act of 2002 in the United States. The requirements of the act aim to enhance corporate governance through measures that will strengthen internal checks and balances and, ultimately, strengthen corporate accountability. Likewise, in March 2004, the European Commission published a proposed directive on suggested auditing rules for corporations within the European Union (EU). The proposal has as its purpose to begin to establish a base so that shareholders can rely on the accuracy of audited corporate accounts. It is part of a larger plan for reforming corporate governance and contains similar suggested approaches and language that were part of the U.S.-led legislation in the Sarbanes-Oxley Act of 2002. Corporations throughout the European Union will need to ensure they have business process management procedures, and governance. Governance framework and criteria are critical in today's business environment especially when the enterprise is global and extends to other entities.

*Governance* is often defined as ethical corporate behavior by directors or others in the wealth creation process, and how these persons provide stewardship over the business of the entity. Specifically, governance is "A set of responsibilities and practices exercised by the board and executive management with the goal of providing strategic direction, ensuring that objectives are achieved, ascertaining that risks are managed appropriately and verifying that the enterprise's resources are used responsibly."[6]

In the extended enterprise environment, ecosystem performance needs to focus on strategy over ownership as a unifying concept. Performance will then be driven from the strategy. Linkages are established between business objectives and IT and the approach is synchronized to create an overall business architecture.

IT governance is the responsibility of the board of directors and executive management. It consists of the leadership and organizational structures and processes that ensure that an organization's IT sustains and extends its strategies and objectives. The enterprise has several challenges and concerns:

- Aligning IT strategy with the business strategy
- Cascading strategy and goals down into the enterprise
- Providing organizational structures that facilitate the implementation of strategy and goals

- Insisting that an IT control framework be adopted and implemented
- Measuring IT's performance

Effective and timely measures aimed at addressing these top management concerns need to be promoted by the governance layer of an enterprise. Hence, boards and executive management need to extend governance, already exercised over the enterprise, to IT.

Successful enterprises have integrated IT and business strategies, culture, and ethics to optimize information value, attain business objectives, and capitalize on technologies even in the highly competitive global environment. In fact, IT, long considered solely an enabler of an enterprise's strategy, is now regarded as an integral part of that strategy. Chief executive officers (CEOs), chief technology officers (CTOs), chief financial officers (CFOs), and chief information officers (CIOs) alike agree that strategic alignment between IT and the enterprise mission is a critical success factor. The recognition of the CIO and CTO as business partners along with the CFO and CEO is a key milestone on the path to effective realization of an effective governance structure.

## GOVERNANCE OFFICER

Governance structure can only be implemented when a knowledge portal is provided for sound two-way communication among partners of the extended enterprise and a project governance officer is assigned for coordination and monitoring of knowledge sharing activities. Chapter 5 of the text deals with governance issues related to the extended enterprise environment. It focuses squarely on the issues of governance challenges and approaches to structure, including the governance criteria needed to effectively participate in the changed business environment. There are various maturity models presented for the criteria, as well as a comparison of various global excellence models in existence.

## ENTERPRISE ARCHITECTURE: FRAMEWORK AND IMPLEMENTATION

Enterprise architectures are commonly viewed as being for the IT department, and IT applications as back-office functions. However, with Internet technology, organizations began to experience problems with their enterprise architecture. These organizations were finding that the architecture was hindering their business rather than supporting it. They recognized the need for a new enterprise architecture to support their business. This new approach involves focusing on a single unifying concept—the business architecture. The business architecture removes the boundaries between business and IT planning. The business architecture dictates the shape of the IT environment and supports effective IT governance.

On the basis of understanding the business, an enterprise architecture can be pictured as the knowledge that defines the business, the information necessary to operate the business, the technologies necessary to support the business operations, and the overall processes necessary for implementing IT, all responding to the changing needs of the business. From the information technology architecture perspective, the components will include a plan for the set of resources and services that the business applications will utilize. Chapter 6 presents the concepts, a sample architecture approach, issues for the CIO, a maturity model for dealing with enterprise architecture, as well as a sample maturity model for IT governance. Appendix A presents a series of questions that should be considered by senior management in delivering overall governance for the extended enterprise.

## REFERENCE WORKS

The IT Governance Institute recognizes the following works as providing the basis for the governance model in the extended enterprise:

- *Balanced Scorecard.* Developed by Harvard professors Kaplan and Norton, the balanced scorecard is a framework that helps translate vision and strategy into a coherent set of performance measures.

- *Board Briefing on IT Governance.* Developed by the IT Governance Institute, this document, now in its second edition, delivers high-level guidance to boards of directors on the importance of IT governance, questions to ask, and what can be done to address the challenge.

- *Capability Maturity Model (CMM).* Developed by the Software Engineering Institute, this model provides the principles and practices that make up software process maturity, providing guidance to those that want to improve their software processes.

- *COSO Enterprise Risk Management Framework.* A conceptual framework providing integrated principles, common terminology and practical implementation guidance supporting entities' programs to develop or benchmark their enterprise risk management processes.

- *European Framework for Quality Management (EFQM).* A framework excellence model, endorsed by the European Commission. It is designed to improve services and products/manufacturing quality in organizations.

- *Enterprise Architecture.* A roadmap developed by the U.S. government to assist in achieving its mission through the optimal performance of its business processes within an efficient IT environment.

- *ISO 9001-2000.* Standards published by the International Standards Organization, and used for establishing a management system that provides confidence in the conformance of a product or service to established or specified quality requirements.

- *Malcolm Baldrige National Quality Criteria Framework.* A framework that was developed in the United States, and has evolved from a quality focus to performance excellence. It covers leadership, strategic planning, customer and market focus, information and analysis, human resource focus, process management and business.

- *OECD Principles of Corporate Governance.* Principles developed to assist OECD and non-OECD governments in their efforts to evaluate and improve the legal, institutional, and regulatory framework for corporate governance in their countries and to provide guidance and suggestions for stock exchanges, investors, corporations, and other parties that have a role in the process of developing good corporate governance.

- *Technical Reference Model.* A common vocabulary so that the diverse entities can better coordinate their acquisition, development, interoperability, and support of their information systems, authored by the CIO Council of the U.S. government. The CIO Council is a group of agency and departmental CIOs of the U.S. government. The purpose of the group is to ensure sharing and alignment of IT resources across the far-reaching parts of the government.

Regular monitoring of activities against an established extended enterprise governance model is essential to ensure that an entity's governance is proceeding as originally planned. Unless an extended enterprise governance model is implemented, an enterprise runs the risk of its business objectives not being in alignment with both its activities and utilization of resources. An enterprise's executive management and auditors are all likely to have roles and responsibilities in ensuring effective governance in the extended enterprise.

## LOOKING FORWARD

This extended enterprise governance approach has effective links with the IT Governance Institute's other control models: COBIT® *(Control Objectives for Information and related Technology)*, and CONCT *(Control Objectives for Net Centric Technology)*.

The model for extended enterprise governance is also consistent with the recommendations of the COSO Report,[7] Committee of Sponsoring Organizations Internal Control Framework, as well as other well-respected control frameworks such as COCO,[8] Cadbury,[9] and King.[10]

Most businesses will move to a new enterprise architecture where business and IT functions will combine and form the business architecture. There will be a board level sponsor responsible for ensuring that business architecture objectives are defined and met. The chief information officers (CIOs) and the chief technology officers (CTOs) must understand that they no longer own the enterprise architecture; instead, they should aim to deliver IT solutions to meet the larger business needs of the enterprise.

## NOTES

1. Michael Hammer, *Beyond Reengineering* (New York: Harper Business, 1996).
2. Kevin Kelly, *New Rules for the New Economy* (New York: Viking Penguin, 1998).
3. Ibid.
4. Therese Morin, Ken Devansky, Card Little, and Craig Petrun, *Information Leadership—A Government Executive's Guide* (PricewaterhouseCoopers, LLP, 1999).
5. Jorge Lopez, *Strategy of Acceleration: Time to Change Culture and Architecture,* Gartner Research, July 29, 2002, www.gartnerg2.com/research/rpt-0702-0124.asp.
6. *Board Briefing on IT Governance,* 2nd edition (Rolling Meadows, IL: IT Governance Institute, October 2003).
7. Committee of Sponsoring Organizations of the Treadway Commission (COSO), *Enterprise Risk Management Framework* (Jersey City, NJ: American Institute of Certified Accountants, September 2004).
8. *Criteria of Control,* Canadian Institute of Chartered Accountants, 1995.

9. The committee on the Financial Aspects of Corporate Governance set up in May 1991 by the U.K. Financial Reporting Council, the London Stock Exchange, and the U.K. Accountancy profession was chaired by Sir Adrian Cadbury and produced the report commonly known as the Cadbury Report.

10. *The King Report on Corporate Governance for South Africa,* 2001.

# 1

# EXTENDED ENTERPRISES

## CHANGE AGENTS IN THE EXTENDED ENTERPRISE ENVIRONMENT

Global connectivity and the changes it supports are perhaps the most significant component of the current paradigm realignment. Through connectivity with the Internet, an enterprise is now able to conduct business anywhere, anytime—eclipsing the traditional constraints of time, distance, and location. This has paved the way for the current global outsourcing and offshoring. The Internet is also enabling a transformation of business processes and procedures. This transformation is occurring in a series of phases starting from the availability of information for marketing and improved communication to the evolution of virtual markets, to the fulfillment of orders and payments and, finally, to after-sale support of customers. As enterprises commit resources to transform into extended enterprises, education and training must be provided to employees, business partners, suppliers, and customers to close any gaps between required strategic objectives and current skill levels. Furthermore, these phases are not necessarily contiguous, as ongoing business and technology developments are creating the need for constant reinvention of business processes within each phase.

Here are some of the early change drivers that have paved the shift toward the extended enterprise approach of doing business:

- Customer empowerment
- Globalization of markets
- Visionary leadership

- Dramatic cost reduction
- Reduced time-to-market
- Improved logistics and delivery
- E-business
- Global workforce outsourcing and offshoring

## Customer Empowerment

Global connectivity has turned the traditional supplier-customer relationship upside down. The assembly line approach to production technologies is rapidly giving way to customer-driven production processes, which in large part are enabled by the Internet and the use of extended partners. Customers can pull down information as and when needed and reach out instantly to a multitude of suppliers. Accordingly, suppliers must transform their business processes to respond to the customer as the one-to-one business driver—both in their marketing and in their provision of ongoing customer service. These changes apply to both business-to-business markets and business-to-consumer markets. One example of the customer-driven production process is Dell's ability to configure equipment to match the needs of an individual buyer, thus forever changing the nature of personal computer (PC) retailing. This customer empowerment approach has now been adopted by other PC manufacturers, such as IBM and Hewlett Packard. In the business-to-business venue, most of the automotive manufacturers now are reaching out to extend themselves as they do business with suppliers, and so on. They, in turn, are positioning themselves out toward the customer (dealerships and purchasers).

## Globalization of Markets

Interconnectivity through the use of the Internet is driving competition, lowering costs, and reinforcing the shift to globalization. By interconnecting buyers and sellers without geographic constraints and taking advantage of the extended environment, nimble players can gain rapid market share at the cost of well-entrenched incumbents. Over the last several years, there has been some rather drastic dismantling of the late 1990s business model espoused by a click-only strategy, toward embracing more of a click and mortar strategy. However, this new interconnectivity has created an opening of the global markets to even the smallest of players. The characteristics of products/services have a large influence on whether the buyers and sellers can interconnect without geographic constraints. The click and mortar strategy is not always easy for small players, because it may require a large investment for infrastructures, such as warehouse and distribution centers. Small players may seek partnering with other players to stay in the game. The rapid market-share growth that was attained by e-portals (gateways to a multitude of suppliers), such as Amazon.com, attests to the impact that new entrants can generate in almost any market segment, if the focus on the customer is unrelenting. This partnering will continue to create interdependencies as never before.

## Visionary Leadership

Senior leaders ensure the creation of strategies, systems, logistics, and processes for achieving the necessary enterprise excellence. In the new economy, leadership needs to work to encourage all employees to contribute, learn, innovate, and be creative. Just as the customer has been empowered, so must the employee. Leaders need to serve as role models; and with the shift to the global market, the need for cost reductions, and reduced time-to-market, the new leadership must be able to swiftly reinforce both values and expectations as they form and sustain the enterprise's culture.

## Dramatic Cost Reduction

Physical inventories have always been a major cost component of old businesses. In the emerging business model, certain businesses will seek to maintain virtual inventories by directly linking to suppliers. In turn, this will lead to a reduction in required inventory levels, as the supplier can ship directly to the customer. In other businesses, such as manufacturers, these entities also seek to lower inventories by having suppliers maintain component inventories at nearby locations, or they are involved in collaborative product design and coordinated production scheduling with other enterprises. In addition, new ways of doing business means many of the traditional distribution approaches associated with showrooms, catalog production, and so on, are set to decline. These trends may enable cost reductions and provide an engine of growth for the global economy into the future. Cost reductions may also occur from customers contacting suppliers directly, but there are some additional costs to be faced in providing sound, adequate, and robust security over customer access to the enterprise's networks and applications and in storing greater volumes of information for customers to access.

## Reduced Time to Market

Minimal time to market is no longer just a competitive advantage but a competitive *necessity* for survival. Through collaborative product development and knowledge sharing with business partners, time to market can be successfully reduced. In some cases, a customer can actually become involved in product development, such as software and computer hardware development. For example, software companies now often release the beta version of a new software product on their website, thus allowing customers to download the software for free and provide timely feedback to the software developers. This not only benefits the developer, it also helps to create an increased future demand for the product.

## Improved Logistics and Delivery

To be successful in Internet commerce, an enterprise must be as effective in the physical world as it is in the electronic arena. Time-value is an essential variable in today's e-business environment and is a critical component of customer service. To accommodate this need, the role of the warehouse itself has changed from being a holding bin to an assembly plant. For example, computer distributors assemble computers from standard parts instead of having assembly by their brand custodian's warehouses. Also, global couriers, such as FedEx, are positioning themselves to become tomorrow's flying assembly plants.

## E-Business

The drivers mentioned provide an indication of some of the emerging trends in the extended enterprise environment. Also, these drivers represent a broad framework for enabling new forms of business, for requiring new strategies for business, and for encouraging the evolution of e-business in the extended enterprise.

To effectively support e-business, organizations must turn inwardly focused processes around to face outward toward customers, trading partners, suppliers, and distributors. The outward-facing applications must include business partners—particularly where interconnections make it possible to do things in ways not previously possible by eliminating time, distance, and location. Current inward-looking applications that may need to be realigned include research and development (R&D), engineering, manufacturing and production, supply chains, marketing, sales, and customer support.

E-business is an infrastructure for a whole new way of doing business and must extend the business processes across organizational boundaries to integrate them with suppliers' and customers' business processes and eradicate unproductive and/or duplicate processes. Whether developing e-business applications in-house or implementing an enterprise resource planning (ERP) package, a holistic approach to business initiatives must be refined for today's entities to have a chance for success in the new extended environment.

## Global Workforce Outsourcing and Offshoring

In the age of global specialization, each piece of the enterprise must add value to the overall business. Currently, there is an emerging sense of comparative advantage where businesses or parts thereof are focusing on what they have competence in and do well and outsourcing the other functions to partners to overcome any comparative disadvantages in the global market. Examples of this can be seen in organizations such as IBM, Dell, and Sony. All three are using this model to enhance their core competitive model. Responsiveness is needed to change and to adapt to conditions. Speed and responsiveness require distributed actions, which could go beyond an organization's borders and extend to global workforce sourcing including co-location or even offshoring to other countries.

The idea of global workforce outsourcing/offshoring or sharing services is an important shift from the old economy to the extended enterprise. A global workforce, if implemented correctly, can play a critical role in boosting shareholder value and permit an organization to focus on areas that are part of their competencies and critical to inventing, manufacturing, and selling. It allows something of importance to a business to be performed by others that may have the expertise and may do it better, more economically, or in a more appropriate location. Self-sufficiency could be too costly.

## PARADIGM SHIFT IN THE BUSINESS ENVIRONMENT/CHANGES IN PROCESSES

Michael Hammer, one of the world's leading authors on business strategy, states in his book, *Beyond Reengineering,* that as global competition grows, organizations are turning to virtual integration, which lets them concentrate solely on the processes in which they know they can be world-class, and have a competitive advantage. They will then rely on, or partner with, someone outside the enterprise to perform the rest.[1]

Similarly, Kevin Kelly, a well-respected author on the subject, states, "The final destiny for the future of the company often seems to be the virtual corporation—the corporation as a small nexus with essential functions outsourced to subcontractors. But there is an alternative vision of an ultimate destination—the company that is only staffed by customers. No firm will ever reach that extreme, but the trajectory that leads in that direction is the right one, and any steps taken to shift the balance toward relying on the relationships with customers will prove to be an advantage."[2]

As mentioned earlier, the phenomenon where an organization extends outside its traditional boundaries is commonly described as an *extended enterprise,* a *virtual enterprise,* or even as a *virtually integrated enterprise.* In the diversity of the e-business environment, the greatest benefits for an organization have been attained by those entities that endorsed and embraced this extended enterprise concept, and then adapted it to best fit the environment in which they operate.

In the past, management-led organizations were structured as vertical silos. They typically did everything (R&D, manufacturing, distribution, sales, logistics, and customer relationship management) under one roof. Additionally, the processes that made up the traditional businesses were pointed inward. With competition, organizations began to disperse some of the key business activities to various geographic locations, but still within the same enterprise. Gradually, cost constraints and global competition have forced these organizations to look beyond their internal boundaries—for example, at outsourcing all noncore activities. However, it was not until the advent of the Internet and the related ability to have inter-networked enterprises, that outsourcing could actually be structured into a more strategic focus.

With the rapid proliferation of Internet and web-enabled technologies, customers and other stakeholders expect, and are now able to select, the best quality of products/services offered around the world, thus *world class.* Education of the masses due to the Internet is creating a new value proposition where the old optimization triangle (cost, time, and value) can all be optimized, whereas previously only two of the three (inexpensive and quick with lesser quality) could be accomplished. This shift is now creating an enormous change in how value and services are perceived. Opportunities for enterprises to make significant improvements in productivity, customer service, and quality have never been greater. Increasingly, for enterprises to survive and ensure growth, they must provide world-class products/services without taking into account geographic boundaries. Many organizations are now focusing on their core competencies, or what they can do best, and extending their business processes by teaming with networks of similarly focused partners and sharing services.

Partners of an extended enterprise share a sense of co-destiny, thus nurturing high-quality collaboration. More and more, organizations are realizing that they cannot innovate in isolation. To the contrary, network technologies now available enable a level of organizational agility where the key to growth lies in the forging of effective virtual inter-organizational relationships. Through this agility, enterprises can deliver their products/services to their customers and business partners quickly, efficiently, and at the same or higher level of expected quality, but at lower cost. A paradigm shift has occurred with these emerging practices in the business environment, as would be expected when transferring to meet the demands of the extended enterprise.

The extended enterprise structure can best be described as a combination of extended value chains. Enterprises today are positioning themselves not as simple, one-dimensional value chains, but as value networks that pull together capabilities in a nonlinear fashion. Enterprises can participate in multiple extended enterprises and provide capabilities across many value chains. However, these may add a new level of complexity in the interacted relationships of the new partners of the value chain.

To achieve coherence and manage the complexity and change inherent in multiple e-business applications, each partner of an extended enterprise needs to share objectives, goals, and/or expectations of the group. This environment is not bliss: cooperation is still competition, even between members of the same value chain. Co-destiny, if not properly managed, may end brutally for competitive reasons. In addition, partners have their own shareholder and stakeholder expectations that must be managed. The rule for intellectual property must be considered in the areas of collaborative work on virtual enterprises to ensure that each enterprise cannot display their skills without compliance to these rules. Current legal, accounting, and related structures do not provide any solution for this extended enterprise other than contract-based agreements for trade transactions.

## SUMMARY

The examples in this chapter have presented a broad spectrum of ideas and change drivers that are impacting businesses and governmental entities as they focus on conducting commerce in a truly networked and global environment. The one biggest agent impacting organizations that are doing, or looking to do, business in the extended environment is customer empowerment. The shift has truly created the need to turn the internal processes of an enterprise outward, toward the customer, if one truly expects to be successful in the twenty-first century. The proliferation and acceptance by the customer of the Internet, and its associated technologies, has created a fundamental shift in what is possible, as well as what is expected by the customer. These expectations will have to be met, and sometimes, entities will not be able to do everything themselves, nor move quickly enough themselves, thus the need to partner with others, or extend the enterprise.

## NOTES

1. Michael Hammer, *Beyond Reengineering* (New York: HarperCollins, 1996).
2. Kevin Kelly, *New Rules for the New Economy* (New York: Viking Penguin, 1998).

# 2

# STRATEGY: CHALLENGE FOR THE EXTENDED ENTERPRISE

## BUSINESS STRATEGY CHALLENGE

Strategy planning, under traditional organizational management, generally focuses on establishing defensible strategic positions by setting organizational scopes, acquiring or building assets, and establishing a balanced and authorized set of priorities. In a low-velocity market, this emphasis was indeed acceptable, as change was slower and more predictable. However, in today's high-velocity markets and rapidly changing global environment, strategic position can be quickly eroded. Therefore, where managers once annually considered reconfiguring their resources to build a new strategy position more pivotal to overall corporate performance, now many organizations are generating a greater and more frequent focus on an ongoing strategic process. Developing a successful and sustainable strategy requires continual alignment of an organization's internal processes with its customer-value proposition. Further, management is focusing on agility and the ability to capture synergies and use them as part of a proactive, rather than a defensive, strategy. They are looking at strategies emerging from the individual entrepreneurial business perspective. They require environmental analysis as a basis for managing their own group dynamics. This emphasis is critical, since it is becoming increasingly difficult to predict which competencies or strategies will be successful and the length of time during which they will be valid.

Organizations that have moved toward the extended enterprise concepts have adapted a perspective on strategy that is focused on competition and creates a continuing flow of temporary and shifting competitive advantages. Michael Dell, CEO of Dell Computer Corporation, once commented, "The only constant in our business is that everything is changing . . . constant challenge, so we have to be ahead of the game."[1] However, creating a series of shifting advantages is time challenging. It requires effective decision making at the unit level to improve business strategy, at the multi-business level to create collective strategy and cross-business synergies, and at the corporate level to articulate the corporate mission, vision, and major redirection points in strategic directions.

To achieve great strategic outcomes in the extended enterprise, visionary leaders must be encouraged to emerge, thus enabling innovation. The following are key points for inclusion in setting strategy for the extended enterprise environment:

- Being aware of new enterprise risk structures, including new regulatory challenges
- Developing strategy with a continual focus on creating value through innovation (value innovation)
- Transforming internal governance strategy to match the changing needs of the external and internal environments facing the enterprise
- Focusing on new internal governance challenges
- Making strategy a continual process—evolving, linking, and patching (bridging between new initiatives to achieve holistic results)
- Sharing the knowledge required to govern the enterprise effectively through use of a knowledge portal
- Managing knowledge for more effective communication and directly actionable outcomes

## NEW ENTERPRISE RISK MANAGEMENT STRUCTURES

In today's competitive business environment, entities are faced with rapid changes and uncertainties created by new technologies, regulations, and organization restructuring, to name a few. This has presented a new challenge in terms of risk management and strategic choices. For example, an entity's strategy is to expand its focus to other lines of business. Although such a business decision would enhance growth, it also creates uncertainty resulting from inability to accurately determine the likelihood that potential events will occur. This might adversely impact an enterprise's ability in achieving its objectives.

*Enterprise risk management* can be effectively applied across the enterprise in strategy setting. The amount of risk that an enterprise is willing to accept in pursuit of goals is directly related to the enterprise's strategy, and is addressed during strategy setting. The desirable return from strategy, in practice, is commonly aligned with the established acceptable risk level or risk tolerance. Enterprise risk management facilitates senior management in selecting strategies that are consistent with the established risk tolerance.

As stated in the Committee of Sponsoring Organizations' (COSO) Enterprise Risk Management Framework published in September 2004, "Events with a potentially negative impact represent risks . . ." and "events with potentially positive impact may offset negative impacts or they may represent opportunities."[2] Potential events that may have an impact on an entity must be adequately defined and identified and must include factors that may affect strategy implementation and achievement of objectives. Such factors could be internal and/or external. Internal factors are those established by management and represent management's philosophy and operating style. Examples of internal factors are infrastructure, personnel, process, and technology. External event factors, by contrast, are those occurring outside the entity and are outside the entity's control. Examples of external factors include economic, political, and technological events.

## NEW REGULATORY COMPLIANCE CHALLENGE

A critical factor to an enterprise's success is to ensure business objectives are aligned with the selected strategy relative to all of its activities. One of the enterprise's mission, strategy, and related objectives is meeting its obligations as it relates to regulatory compliance. Introduction of new or revised legislation would greatly impact an entity's strategies and governance responsibilities. For instance, the passing of the Sarbanes-Oxley Act of 2002 by the U.S. legislature has significantly impacted entities' strategy and related objectives as well as the corporate governance perspective. Select enterprises identified in the Act must ensure that they have business process management procedures in place to respond to the legislation. Along these same lines, in March 2004, The European Commission published a proposed directive on auditing rules for corporations within the European Union (EU), which included a plan for reforming corporate governance similar to the Sarbanes-Oxley Act of 2002. The following is a brief description of the Sarbanes-Oxley Act of 2002 in the United States as it relates to corporate governance, and then a brief explanation of the European Commission's directive.

## Sarbanes-Oxley Act of 2002

The Sarbanes-Oxley Act of 2002, which was passed into law in the United States, has fundamentally changed the business and regulatory environment. The act aims to enhance corporate governance through measures that will strengthen internal checks and balances and, ultimately, strengthen corporate accountability. It contains 11 main sections. It is important to emphasize that one of those subsections, 404, does not merely require organizations to establish and maintain an adequate internal control structure, but also requires them to assess and report on its effectiveness on an annual basis. This distinction is significant.

The Sarbanes-Oxley Act demonstrates a firm resolve by the U.S. Congress to improve corporate responsibility. It was created to restore investor confidence in U.S. public markets, which was damaged by business scandals and lapses in corporate governance. Although it and supporting regulations have rewritten the rules for accountability, disclosure, and reporting, the act's many pages of legalese support a simple premise: good corporate governance and ethical business practices are no longer optional.

For those organizations that have begun the compliance process, it has quickly become apparent that IT plays a vital role in the internal control assessment process. Systems, data, and infrastructure components are critical to the financial reporting process. The nature and characteristics of a company's use of information technology in its information system affect the company's internal control over financial reporting.

To this end, IT professionals, especially those in executive positions, need to be well versed in internal control theory and practice to meet the requirements of the Sarbanes-Oxley Act. CIOs must now take on these challenges:

- Enhancing their knowledge of internal control
- Understanding their organization's overall Sarbanes-Oxley compliance plan
- Developing a compliance plan to specifically address IT controls
- Integrating this plan into the overall Sarbanes-Oxley compliance plan[3]

## European Commission Directive

In March 2004, the European Commission published a proposed directive on auditing rules for corporations within the European Union (EU). The proposal, which will need to go through and be approved by the European Parliament and the Council of Ministers, has as its purpose to begin to establish a base so that shareholders can rely on the accuracy of audited corporate accounts. It is part of a larger plan for reforming corporate governance and contains similar approaches and language that were part of the U.S.-led legislation in the Sarbanes-Oxley Act of 2002. Corporations will need to ensure they have business process management procedures, including audit trails and document management, in place and are ready to respond to the proposed European Union auditing rules directive. Key provisions are expected to cover, among others: registration, public oversight, quality assurance, international standards, audit communities, and internal control reporting. This regulatory and compliance movement is bound to continue its swath across the world.[4]

## DEVELOPING STRATEGY WITH VALUE INNOVATION

Traditionally, competitive forces have been a key building block of strategy in theory and practice. Strategy, in this context, defines the way entities build advantages over the competition. It has been the strategic objective for many organizations and, in itself, there is nothing wrong with this objective. Organizations need to show distinct advantages over the competition to sustain them in the marketplace. Leaders typically assess what competitors do and then strive to do better. Such strategic thinking regresses toward the competition because organizations may be making tremendous efforts to be better than competitors. The end results may not be more than incremental improvement.

The issue of innovation is not considered an end in itself or the ultimate solution to current business systems. However, in the extended enterprise, leaders in value innovation are among the most rapidly growing organizations. According to W. Chan Kim and Renee Mauborgne, "Strategy driven by the competition usually has three latent, unintended efforts. They are:

1. Imitative, not innovative, approaches to the market where companies accept what competitors are doing and simply strive to do it better.

2. Companies act reactively, resulting in time and talent that are unconsciously absorbed by responding to daily competitive moves rather than creating growth opportunities.

3. A company's understanding of emerging mass markets and changing customer demands becomes hazy."[5]

In the extended enterprise, strategy focuses on what is called *value innovation,* and has become a cornerstone of the enterprise's mission. It is quite different from building layers of competitive advantage and it strives to do more than outperform the competition. Value innovation makes competition irrelevant by offering fundamentally new and superior buyer value in existing markets and by enabling a leap of capability to create new markets. The steady growth of organizations, such as The Home Depot in home improvement retail, SAP in business application software, and Charles Schwab & Co. in investment and brokerage account management, is not based solely on big commitments to the latest technology. These companies are committed to their pursuit of innovation outside a conventional context. Their leadership's central focus is squarely rooted in pursuing innovation as value. Another value innovator, Wal-Mart, has become one of the world's largest organizations in both revenue and employee head count through understanding both the fundamentals of its industry and how to use innovative processes to achieve competitive advantage. It is also one of the biggest believers in the extended enterprise concept. In all of these examples, technology certainly is an integral part of that innovation.

*Value without innovation* tends to focus on improving the buyer's net benefit or creation on an incremental scale. Innovation without value can result in too strategic or too technology-driven or too futuristic a focus. Value innovation is not the same as value creation; instead, it anchors innovation with buyer value. Knowledge and ideas (human creative input) are the major inputs for value innovation. It can occur in any organization and at any time in a sustainable manner with a proper process.

*Value innovation* is the essence of strategy in the extended enterprise and knowledge economy. Senior leaders need to foster the development and use of proper tactics to stimulate value innovation. They in turn must prolong and maximize an innovation's profit-making potential and must support its strategy. After a value innovation initiative is created, line-of-business extensions and continuous improvements can maximize profits before the next value innovation initiative is launched. Senior leaders should always ask: What can I do to further my mission? How does this move me closer to my vision? These two questions are fundamental to value innovation.

## TRANSFORMING INTERNAL GOVERNANCE STRATEGY

Internal governance refers to the wealth creation processes inside diversified multinational extended enterprises, and relates to the roll-down of the external corporate governance responsibilities and practices exercised by the board and executive management to the business units and to the relationships with strategic external partners of the extended enterprise. There are three important aspects that relate to internal governance:

1. Pursuing growth and innovation
2. Cultivating strong corporate business-unit relationships and ethics
3. Fostering interbusiness unit linkages

The rate of change in organizations, and in the extended enterprise environment in particular, has been so rapid that many entities have not been able to transform their internal governance strategy or processes to meet the new changes. Although organizations recognize the need for rapid transformation of their internal governance, most of the problems confronted are in determining how to accomplish that transformation. It is not because of the constraints in employing either knowledge or globalization of economies and financial constraints, IT (data warehouse, Internet, etc.) and business technologies (customer relationship management, supply chain management, etc.). The problem, of course, is that shortfalls in the processes mentioned previously cannot be attributed to tangible resource constraints.

The constantly changing nature of customers' expectations, age, income levels, regional spread, and knowledge base have profound implications. Business has to become proactive in relating to its consumers as they gain access to more information on the business's expertise and start exercising new options opened to them by access to information. With the introduction of Net-centric technologies, the Internet enables virtually endless connectivity where everything can be connected to everything else with one click. As stated by Kevin Kelly, "The distinguishing characteristics of networks are that they contain no clear center and no clear outside boundaries. Within a network, everything is potentially equidistant from everything else."[6] In many ways, customers are in charge and the separation between customers and an organization's employees is slowly dissipating. Managers face competitive challenges such as those described in the following paragraphs.

The traditional value chain channel structures are being confronted. Manufacturers are now in direct contact with the end users by eliminating intermediaries, such as wholesalers and distributors. Organizations are gaining increasingly sophisticated knowledge of their consumers, and are strategically retaining more information on each individual to allow the enterprise to serve them better (micro-marketing). Selling and administrative costs, as a percentage of sales, are likely to decline in most organizations.

Learning how to harmonize traditional technologies with new ones is a challenge. For example, consumer electronics entities such as Sony Corporation need to learn to harmonize what used to be the separate domains of telecommunications, computing, and software and combine these capabilities seamlessly. Technology products such as cellular phones, pagers, personal digital assistants, and Web TV are examples of the results of such integration.

The traditional industry boundaries are quickly disappearing among telecommunications, computing, and consumer electronics industries. The personal computer today might be serving as a bridge between those three traditional industries, and it is the personal digital assistant (PDA) or other such devices that will most likely perform such a function in the future.

The transformation of traditional industry boundaries to the extended enterprise is also taking place in other industries such as investment, insurance, and banking. These changes suggest that the business models developed to compete in a traditional industry structure are becoming less and less relevant in the extended enterprise.

The life cycle of products and services are becoming dramatically shortened and are approaching a zero cycle. Senior management now expects competing products to be produced and appear almost immediately. One of the issues caused by this is that it means that the organization must gain volume rapidly to amortize its investment. Scaling up the value chain, supply chain, distribution, and marketing has been a critical competitive capability. This imposes huge new demands on organizations. Access to a responsive supplier base, global logistics and flexible manufacturing systems and a global workforce are becoming new sources of competitive advantage. For example, it is possible to get things accomplished in information technology 24/7 today, which is an incredible strategic asset for many enterprises to differentiate themselves from competitors.

All established organizations are faced with these competitive challenges, but these challenges are often viewed as loss of market share, unattractive products and profit declines as the result of inefficiencies rather than of the rapid change in the competitive landscape. Management must recognize the futility of old solutions and begin to recognize the new internal governance issues that competitive challenges are generating.

## NEW INTERNAL GOVERNANCE CHALLENGE

Some internal governance challenges arising in the extended enterprise include the following:

- Strategy in this evolving environment involves convincing customers of what the future could be and then shaping and delivering that future. The goal is to create new competitive space.
- Management, in general, must obtain and maintain a level of knowledge of IT disciplines and technologies.
- Organizational environment must resemble a network of distributed intelligence and the future universal usage of this network.
- There is a need for management to think globally, regionally, and locally all at the same time.
- Innovations emanate from both the organizational and business unit levels.
- Convergence of technologies requires that managers rapidly absorb and integrate new knowledge with old as well as reconfiguring all that knowledge into new business opportunities.
- Information must be seen as an organizational resource and shared among the management team. It cannot be used as a source of private power.
- A different pace will permeate all aspects of an organization's activity, from reducing cycle time to exploiting global markets.

Management approaches used within an enterprise also require reinvention or renovation to focus on how the organization's management must proceed with innovations both to compete and to create wealth. Management must step out of the zone of comfort and into the zone of creating opportunity. Looking at the transformation process, it is clear to see the strategy at its heart identifies challenges, determines their impact on markets, and develops new business models. A successful transformation depends on matching strategic thinking with flawless execution.

## GOVERNANCE CHALLENGE

Good governance involves a set of relationships between an enterprise's management, its board, its shareholders, and other stakeholders. An enterprise's employees, partners, strategic vendors, and other trading partners will all play vital roles in contributing to the long-term success, viability, and sustainability of the enterprise. In a similar yet different role, local and national governments will have a critical responsibility for shaping an effective regulatory framework that provides for sufficient flexibility to allow markets to function effectively and to respond to expectations of shareholders and other stakeholders. Although the OECD has outlined these issues in its draft document, it will always be up to each particular government as well as the individual enterprise to decide exactly how they intend to apply these principles in developing their own frameworks for good governance. A one-size-fits-all approach should not be exercised. As the OECD points out, good overall governance has been, and should be, the domain of each enterprise. However, as mentioned in the April 2004 OECD governance principles, stakeholders must be closely considered when dealing with the overall governance model and there needs to be a strengthening of board oversight over management. In the extended environment, this is more critical than ever when considering the incentive of the market integrity and overall economic performance. With enterprises relying on outside partners as never before, enterprises need to work this approach into their best practices.[7]

## BRIDGING THE GAP BETWEEN THE INFORMATION TECHNOLOGY ORGANIZATION AND INTERNAL CLIENTS

As part of the alignment process between business and the IT functions, both the IT organization and the business units and process owners must share the responsibility. The IT Governance Institute identified the following items to help bridge the gap:

- Monitor IT performance
- Take into account stakeholder values when setting and approving strategy
- Direct the processes that implement strategy
- Align IT and business strategies, an imperative
- Ensure the results are acted upon[8]

To further support the need to bridge the gap, Susan Dallas provided the following:

- Match the governance initiative with the decision-making style of the enterprise

- Align decision-making authority with the domain
- Integrate the governance mechanisms and evolve them
- Clarify stakeholders' role
- Measure the effectiveness of IT governance
- Facilitate the evolution of IT governance[9]

## MAKING STRATEGY A CONTINUAL PROCESS: COEVOLVING AND PATCHING

A past article in the *Harvard Business Review* stated, "Capturing cross-business synergies is the heart of corporate strategies . . . the promise of synergy is a prime rationale for the existence of the multi-business corporation. . . . Companies that actually achieve synergies when their managers have mastered a corporate strategic process are called *coevolving.*"[10] Another *Harvard Business Review* article, "Patching: Restitching Business Portfolios in Dynamic Markets," stated, " . . . Organizations must have flexible structures. They must respond quickly to increased change . . . Patching is a means of achieving flexibility."[11] The article also explains how to respond flexibly to changing markets through the use of patching.

Coevolving is a sound concept, as is continuous evolution. Both involve routine but dynamic changes to the web of collaborative links among businesses to exploit new opportunities for synergies and strategic growth and to delete those that are no longer valid. The use and application of coevolving is absolutely critical in the extended enterprise, as it enables an organization to quickly meet and adapt to change, as well as to maintain economies of scale and rapid cross-business learning. As things are changing inside the physical boundaries of an entity, they are changing just as fast outside of those boundaries. This concept also refers to reconnecting the collaborative links among businesses as markets and businesses evolve, driving synergies by way of multi-business teams. Patching is referred to as the frequent remapping of business to fit changing market opportunities. Patching and coevolving create a dynamic strategic business process on an ongoing basis, as the business evolves. It is quite different from the traditional strategy process and collaboration where strategic positioning analysis is performed periodically.

For example, under the traditional collaboration business structure, collaboration often takes the form of frozen links among static businesses. There is minimal collaboration between businesses and business partners. Under coevolution, the form of collaboration shifts among evolving businesses and there is no set format in terms of collaboration. The objectives for traditional collaboration are primary efficiency and economies of scope while the objectives for coevolution focus on growth, agility, and economies of scope. The focus of traditional collaboration is content of collaboration while coevolution includes the number of collaboration links. When using traditional collaboration, the corporate role often drives collaboration. In contrast, under coevolution the corporate role sets the collaborative context. The business role under traditional collaboration takes the form of executing collaboration, and under coevolution the business role is drive and executive collaboration. Under traditional collaboration, performance is measured against budget, previous year's experience, or like business performance. Coevolution measures performance against competitors in growth, share, and profit. If the performance increased by 30 percent in terms of growth and profits against the previous year's experience, the matrix would be good under the traditional collaboration. However, if the like industries or competitors' performance is averaging 40 percent increase in growth and profit for the same period, the internal year over year matrix would not be considered good under the coevolution conceptual approach.

## MANAGING KNOWLEDGE FOR BETTER COMMUNICATION: KNOWLEDGE MANAGEMENT

The type of information that will drive organizational innovation may be quite different from that which a manager may generate and use to run operations, such as conventional financial management information. It is much broader in scope, softer in content, and needs to be exploratory in its acquisition process. Business management tends to focus on the past and present facts to predict the future, whereas the gathering of business intelligence requires insights and foresight. New challenges require new responses, and the gathering and the use of business intelligence has been defined as enterprise governance. The innovation and strategy process within each enterprise should be simple, adaptable, and fluid. It should not be broad, vague, mindless, or stale. There is also a danger that what is portrayed as *knowledge management* or another fashionable (magic) solution will offer only a repolished version of existing knowledge within the enterprise (a spin-doctored version).

What is knowledge management? Drs. Robert Kaplan and David Norton, developers of the business balanced scorecard, defined knowledge management as "a systematic approach to find, understand, share and use knowledge to create value."[12] Every organization has some core competitive capabilities. These capabilities link together in a unique way to add to the organization's knowledge structure. Most organizations have embedded basic tenets of learning or knowledge management into the core of business transformation. In simpler terms, these can be referred to as the show-how or know-how used by the enterprise to conduct and direct its activities successfully. However, to use knowledge effectively, one must leverage knowledge to drive business value, learning, and organizational change. As stated in an article by Morten T. Hansen, Nitin Nohria, and Thomas Tierney, "Competitive strategy must drive knowledge management strategy. Executives must be able to articulate why customers buy a company's products or services rather than those of its competitors. What value do customers expect from the company? How does knowledge that resides in the company add value for customers? If a company does not have clear answers to those questions, it should not attempt to choose a knowledge management strategy because it could easily make a bad choice."[13]

Normally, face-to-face communication with a domain knowledge expert, supported by access to a knowledge portal, is the most effective way of sharing knowledge and communicating how the best use of it can be made in practice. The portal access provides ongoing reminders and reference sources when the expert is no longer present.

There are two very different approaches in managing knowledge:

1. Codification or explicit knowledge approach
2. Personalization or implicit knowledge approach

When dealing with the codification approach, information is carefully codified and stored in a database where it can be accessed and used easily by anyone in the organization. Knowledge involves knowing how to extract pieces of information, such as benchmark data or market segmentation analysis for example, out of documents and how to store them in an electronic repository for subsequent wider use. This approach allows many people to search for and retrieve codified information without having to contact the person who was originally responsible for placing it on the repository in the first place.

By contrast, a personalized or implicit approach to sharing knowledge between people within an enterprise focuses on them talking together as individuals to share their knowledge of how-to-do activities rather than accessing knowledge elements stored in a database. To make personalization approaches work, organizations need to build networks of people prepared to share their individual knowledge with their colleagues in the network. Knowledge can be shared not only face-to-face but also over the telephone, by e-mail, via an intranet, or via teleconferencing. Within an enterprise, this sharing can be fostered by transferring people between offices, by creating directories of experts, and by using consultants to assist project teams. Fundamentally, it requires the enterprise to adopt a culture that encourages knowledge sharing in place of knowledge monopolization by those who believe that knowledge is power (this is limited to the power of one—rather than the shared power of the knowledgeable enterprise).

An enterprise's knowledge management approach should reflect its competitive strategy, how it creates value for customers, and how that value supports an economic model. In addition, it should focus on how employees deliver the value and deliver the outcomes expected from the enterprise's economic model. An overall competitive strategy must drive an effective knowledge management strategy. Executives must, for example, be able to spell out why their customers favor their product or services in preference to those of their competitors.

## SHARING KNOWLEDGE THROUGH
## A KNOWLEDGE PORTAL

Knowledge portals are single-point-access software systems designed to provide easy and timely access to information and to support communities of knowledge workers who share common goals. Knowledge and expertise created by knowledge workers as they go about doing their work are captured in a core repository/knowledge portal and made available to their colleagues for strategic activities monitoring such as the state of meeting the extended enterprise vision, value, and strategies. Dashboards describe software systems that provide a user interface for managing projects. Most dashboard software provides indicators or warning messages such as green, yellow, and red to indicate the status of the project being tracked, similar to the displays on an airplane dashboard or cockpit, which the pilot, co-pilot, and navigator use to guide their flight plan.

Information and knowledge derived from continuous environment monitoring should be captured and shared among the partners of the extended enterprise as part of its ongoing strategy process. This sharing can be done through a knowledge portal or dashboard. The information and knowledge related to the area of continuous innovation has a significant probability of adding value and should be monitored.

A conscious, purposeful search for innovation opportunities is required within an enterprise and its partners and in its social and intellectual environment. Such opportunities may arise from any of the following:

- Unexpected occurrences
- Incongruities
- Process needs
- Industry and market changes

The achievement of critical success factors should be closely monitored. If external or internal risks emerge, the enterprises' competitive position may be either threatened or enhanced. The actual gathering of information will be aided by setting up a knowledge information portal to link the enterprise management and other key operational data sources. Monitoring of relationships should also be examined and a database created to interpret the information effectively.

## SUMMARY

Making strategy is a continual process. This certainly is not unique for extended enterprises. Yet, to be effective and successful in the extended environment, one must be able to offer value innovation. Those that are most successful seem to be the ones that are constantly linking, patching, and coevolving. Because the lifecycle of products and services is becoming dramatically shortened, there is a need to reach out and look to partner with those that can add value, and assist in making the offerings world-class. In reaching outside, this has created unique governance issues and challenges. To meet these challenges, entities are turning to portals as ways that they can share information and knowledge with their extended partners, distributors, suppliers, and customers. All this is necessary to ensure the structures measure up and are providing sufficient value when dealing with competitive challenges.

## NOTES

1. D. Narayandas, *Dell Computer Corporation* (Boston: Harvard Business School, case 9-596-058, 1996).
2. Committee of Sponsoring Organizations of the Treadway Commission (COSO), *Enterprise Risk Management Framework* (Jersey City, NJ: American Institute of Certified Accountants, September 2004).

3.  *IT Control Objectives for Sarbanes-Oxley* (Rolling Meadows, IL: IT Governance Institute, April 2004).

4.  Directive of the European Parliament, Proposal, March 2004.

5.  W. C. Kim, R. Mauborgne, "On the Inside Track," *Financial Times* (April 7, 1997), p. 10.

6.  Kevin Kelly, *New Rules for the New Economy* (New York: Viking Penguin, 1998).

7.  OECD Principles of Corporate Governance, April 2004.

8.  *Board Briefing on IT Governance,* 2nd edition (Rolling Meadows, IL: IT Governance Institute, October 2003).

9.  Susan Dallas, "CIO Update: IT Governance Rules to Boost IS Organization and Business Unit Credibility," Gartner Research, *www4.gartner.com/ displaydocument,* December 4, 2002.

10. Katheleen M. Eisenhardt and D. Charles Galunic, "Coevolving: At Last, a Way to Make Synergies Work," *The Harvard Business Review* (January– February 2000).

11. Katheleen M. Eisenhardt and Shonal L. Brown, "Patching: Restitching Business Portfolios in Dynamic Markets," *The Harvard Business Review* (May–June 1999).

12. Robert S. Kaplan and David P. Norton, *The Strategy-Focused Organization* (Boston: Harvard Business School Press, 2001).

13. Morten T. Hansen, Nitin Nohria, and Thomas Tierney, "What Is Your Strategy for Managing Knowledge?" *Harvard Business Review on Organizational Learning* (Boston: Harvard Business School Publishing Press, 2001).

# 3

# VALUE CREATION AND MANAGEMENT OF PERFORMANCE IN THE EXTENDED ENTERPRISE

## VISION AND MISSION

Continuous growth and survival in the highly competitive global environment are the ultimate goals of value creation for an extended enterprise. The desired vision (what we want to be) should be clearly stated and shared among the partners for achieving this objective. This vision will provide the directional compass for partners in a dynamically changing environment. All decisions can then be based on how they forward the vision.

The most powerful vision provides a rich, detailed portrait of the extended enterprise's desired future, including statements of purpose, business definition, performance, customer and stakeholder relations, organizational culture, and even the nature, look, and feel of the work environment. Fundamental and divergent differences in business values based on cultural, legal, or other variances between countries are key issues/challenges.

The mission (why we exist) must be translated to goals and objectives so that the actions of the combined individuals are aligned and supportive of the organization. A continuum exists that is initiated in the broadest sense with the vision, mission, and values of the extended enterprise. The compartmentalization of missions and visions helps the management. It is as if management is saying, "You are a sales guy, so sell—do not worry about from where it is being shipped." Clearly, the compartment you are in needs to build into the overall vision, but departments (geographies, functions, whatever) need to make sure their vision is relevant.

## VALUE CREATION AND STRATEGY IMPLICATIONS

*Values* (what we believe in) are nonnegotiable tenets against which an enterprise measures the worthiness of its choices. They are core to vision: they provide a benchmark for guiding and assessing both team and individual behaviors as well as the ethical standards of the enterprise as a whole. There is a direct correlation between commitment to the stated goals of an enterprise and the collective individual employee's knowledge of personal and enterprise values.

The strategic initiatives are critical aspects of moving forward. An ongoing challenge in extended enterprise management is the development of these strategies, goals, objectives, initiatives, controls, and management metrics for each of the business partner relationships. The extended enterprise management also needs to understand the related strategies of each partner and how the combined specific value chain will assist the extended enterprise in achieving its own predefined metrics.

Running a business in this environment is usually quite complex. The level of difficulty is in direct proportion to the number of partners involved, as well as their cultural and organizational homogeneity. For example, an extended enterprise that involves two partners from the same city sharing common business values is a lot simpler and straightforward than one that involves multiple partners, each from a different continent and each with a unique set of business values.

Resolution of how each participating stakeholder (partner), having different business processes/operational business activities and information systems/information sharing activities, can operate effectively in an extended enterprise environment is critical. The participants need to at least share the necessary information for running the extended enterprise business. In particular, information-sharing activities (two-way or bidirectional communication) among stakeholders is a key success factor in delivering workable enterprise governance.

The creation and management of the value chain can become quite complex due to the participation of multiple parties with different expectations (including the possibility that a business partner might also be a competitor at the same time). Further, the information gathering and delivery mechanisms in the extended enterprise are quite complex.

A good example of an application and use of the extended enterprise environment is the airline industry and the code sharing that takes place among its partners. The consumer deals directly with a reservation structure that integrates information, technology, and value chains, which are all provided by a variety of partners and suppliers that oftentimes includes competitors for the same market space.

## NECESSITY OF A CORE REPOSITORY OF KNOWLEDGE PORTAL

The complexity of the extended enterprise makes the environment foggy and risky. Therefore, the management of each partner should keep focused on their fundamentals such as cost, quality, customer satisfaction, competition monitoring, and inventory levels. (Even the best, such as Cisco, can be adversely affected with overloaded inventories.)

A clear picture should be provided to resolve these complexities. This text suggests the provision of a core repository of information— referred to as a *core knowledge portal* for the extended enterprise.

Implementation of a core information repository is complex work. The guideline suggests a logical Web-based implementation as a knowledge portal. Sufficient resources should be allocated under a well-organized project plan. The project team should manage[1] the work of the project, which typically involves the following:

- Competing demands for: scope, time, cost, risk, and quality
- Stakeholders (partners) with different needs and expectations
- Identified requirements

Many of the processes within a typical project management process are iterative in nature. The scope of an extended enterprise should be flexible to meet the dynamic environment changes and the knowledge portal should have the capability of handling this complexity and flexibility, as illustrated in Exhibit 3.1. Ongoing and periodic monitoring systems over quality, cost, and time of the project should be implemented and risk factors for legal compliance, technology complexity, and culture diversity should be identified and monitored.

## SUGGESTED ARCHITECTURE FOR PERFORMANCE MEASUREMENT

The IT Governance Institute provides architecture for the performance measurement process as illustrated in Exhibit 3.2. This architecture could apply from the oversight governance role to the group as a whole and then to the oversight role at each partner's organizational level, within a partner's governance systems. The oversight role would cascade through the management governance functions at various levels of the enterprise. In this architecture, the governance process starts with

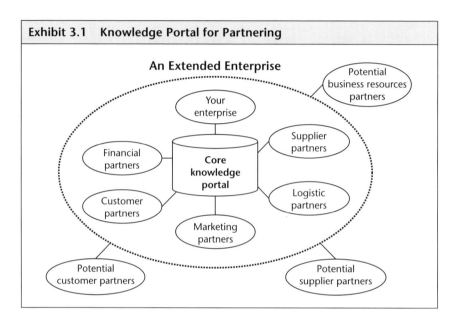

**Exhibit 3.1    Knowledge Portal for Partnering**

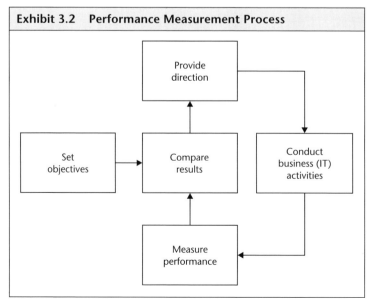

**Exhibit 3.2    Performance Measurement Process**

setting objectives for the extended enterprise, providing initial direction. Moving forward, a continuous loop of performance management is established that is measured and compared to objectives, resulting in redirection of activities where necessary and changes of objectives where appropriate. Thus an enterprise is able to monitor its value creation process. Although objectives are primarily the responsibility of the board of directors and performance measures are the responsibility of management, they should be developed in concert so that the objectives are achievable and the measures represent the objectives correctly.

## DELEGATE AND EMPOWER THROUGH PERFORMANCE MANAGEMENT

Gradual implementation and flexible change of performance measurement through a core knowledge portal are required for an extended enterprise. Nothing new in this for the concept of performance management, but understanding and refreshing the basic function of this management will assist delegation and empowerment through a complicated environment.

The performance measurement of an extended enterprise requires that all those involved in sharing have a clear understanding of their objectives and how they will be achieved. Performance against these objectives needs to be effectively measured at regular intervals to ensure the desired outcomes are being delivered. As a part of the performance measurement process, management has a responsibility to provide value-based reporting. Furthermore, results need to be evaluated and reported to stakeholders. Based on the level of reporting and the results, a gap analysis can be performed to look at where the enterprise is and what needs to be done to achieve an even better performance.

Ultimately, what is measured is what will be attained. The measures that are applied will strongly affect the behavior of all individuals and entities involved. The leading indicators of business performance cannot be found in financial data alone. Quality, customer satisfaction, market share, and other such metrics often reflect the organization's economic condition and growth prospects better than its reported earnings does. Many entities change their performance measurement systems to track nonfinancial measures and reinforce new competitive strategies.

This management process is cyclical and transparent to management. For example, at the beginning of a management process, goals and objectives are defined, responsibilities are assigned, buy-in is obtained, and criteria of performance are developed with the aid of the people responsible for implementation and performance. At the end of the management process, performance is rated against criteria, and then the cycle begins again. Management uses tools such as key performance indicators, critical success factors, and key goal indicators to monitor the process.

One of the unique aspects of the extended enterprise environment is its development, implementation, and use of a knowledge portal for these tools that are structured to include many stakeholders. How to define clear responsibilities and tangible ability for human resources among the partners in the extended enterprise for empowerment is another critical success factor. A suggested example of a standardized qualification evaluation system is the various belt certification systems that are a part of the Six Sigma approach. Further elaboration of Six Sigma is outlined in Appendix B, "Performance Reference Model."

The key difference from traditional environments is that these performance management processes should be transparent to business management in the extended enterprise environment. The performance management should allow the extended enterprise to act in a strategic manner in alignment with its mission and vision, using the overall knowledge gain. Acting on this newfound management cycle, the enterprise is better able to support its decisions and to monitor performance.

## FRAMEWORK FOR MEASUREMENT

In the past, organizations measured the cost of information and technology but often overlooked quantifying their contribution to the program or organizational performance. As the cost of technology increased, management started to require the linkages between information and technology and program results in terms of performance measurement. There are two basic types of measurements:

1. Measures in terms of what customers and stakeholders want
2. Measures of the process of delivering reliable, cost effective, high quality information technology products and services

In terms of what the customer and stakeholders want, the measures generally fall into categories such as better, faster, more reliable business processes that require minimal cost to operate. In addition, the benefits could extend to how the information and technology help management in business decision making and contribute to the organizational strategies.

For the process of delivering reliable, cost effective, and high quality information technology products and services, the measures include benchmark comparisons; operation under allowable budgets and schedules, availability, and other technology related measures. These measures are for managing information and technology.

Frameworks for measurement are tools for organizing and displaying performance measures. Business balanced scorecard is an important tool that an organization uses for all functions and not just information technology. Another framework is Control Objectives for Information and related Technology (CobiT), issued by the IT Governance Institute. The following is a brief discussion of these two frameworks.

## Business Balanced Scorecard: Measures that Drive Performance

The *balanced scorecard approach,* developed by Robert Kaplan and David Norton, has become the most popular new measurement framework in business. Its basic concept is that decision makers need to understand performance in several different perspectives that are important to the success of the organization. Thus, business balanced scorecards with an extended enterprisewide information system equipped by a knowledge portal could be a new strong internal control system, which is able to replace the traditional internal control system.

In the extended enterprise, there are four perspectives needed for a strategy roadmap:

1. Learning and growth
2. Internal business processes
3. Customer perspective
4. Financial performance

In an organization that uses the balanced scorecard for performance measures, senior management (such as the CEO or other top executives) has a scorecard that gives it measures from the previously listed perspectives.

Customer perspective is the heart of an enterprise's strategy. It defines how growth is to be achieved, and the enterprise's value proposition defines the specific strategy to compete for new customers or to increase the share of existing customer business. For the customer, definition of the value proposition is the key to a stronger relationship with the enterprise. Business processes and activities that are internal to the organization need to be established to support delivery of the customer-value proposition. The learning and growth perspective represents the competencies, knowledge, technology, and climate needed to support the business processes and activities internally, as well as to deliver the promised value outcome to the customer. This will result in a better financial position.

If there is a significant change to the environment or in the customer-value proposition offered, the enterprise mission and values may be required to be reviewed and changed accordingly.

The *business balanced scorecard* provides executives and managers complex information at a glance. It consists of a set of measures that gives top managers a fast but comprehensive view of the business. The balanced scorecard includes financial measures that describe the results of actions already taken and complements the financial measures with operational measures on customer satisfaction, internal processes, and the organizational measures that are the drivers of future financial performance. In the extended enterprise environment, managers must be able to view performance in several areas simultaneously. The balanced scorecard allows people in an extended enterprise to think of mission/strategies and to look at the business. In particular it provides answers from four important perspectives:

1. How do we look to shareholders? (financial perspective)
2. How do customers see us? (customer perspective)
3. What internal processes must we excel at? (internal business perspective)
4. How can we continue to improve and create value? (innovation and learning perspective)

Each measure of a balanced scorecard is embedded in a chain of cause-and-effect logic that connects the desired outcomes from the strategy with the drivers that will lead to the strategic outcomes. The strategic map should describe the process for transforming intangible assets into tangible customer and financial outcomes and provide executives with a framework for describing and managing strategy in an extended enterprise. Strategic outcomes should be established that contain a list of desirable outcomes of a mission. Typical desirable outcomes are satisfied shareholders, satisfied customers, effective processes, and a motivated and prepared enterprise workforce.

The business balanced scorecard places strategy and vision squarely at the center and it proactively establishes consensus of goals among the people in an extended enterprise so that people will buy-in and adopt whatever behaviors, and take whatever actions, are necessary to arrive at these goals. The measures are designed to direct people in the extended enterprise toward the overall vision and assist or compel managers to focus on the handful of measures that are most critical. Senior management may know what the end result should be, but they cannot tell people exactly how to achieve that result, if only because the conditions in which partners' people operate are constantly changing.

Current businesses in the extended enterprise are normally covered by agreements between two organizations for integration, coordination, measurement, and awareness. They measure intercompany cross-functional processes using measures that are both functional and financial in nature. The business balanced scorecard can be a vital tool for agreement not only between two organizations but also among partners within the extended enterprises. For further elaboration, see Appendix B, "Performance Reference Model," and the book by Kaplan and Norton, *The Balanced Scorecard: Translating Strategy Into Action.*[2]

## CONTROL OBJECTIVES FOR INFORMATION AND RELATED TECHNOLOGY[3]

Control Objectives for Information and related Technology, *COBIT,* is an approach to internal control and can be used as a framework for organizing and displaying performance measures for different types and levels of information processes. It focuses on work processes and aggregates performance and other data by process and is an excellent framework for organizations that adopt process management instead of more traditional functional management. Performance measurements under COBIT include effectiveness, efficiency, confidentiality, integrity, availability, compliance, and reliability. COBIT includes 34 information processes and provides a comprehensive list of information for developing effective measures for information processes. The model also consists of *Management Guidelines, Control Practices* (the how and why), and *Audit Guidelines,* which provide guidance in analyzing, assessing, and implementing.

COBIT is a tool that allows managers to bridge the gap with respect to business risks, technical issues, and control requirements and to communicate that level of control to stakeholders. It provides good practices across a domain and process framework and presents activities in a manageable and logical structure. The impact on IT resources is highlighted in the COBIT *Framework,* in 34 high-level process statements or control objectives where critical insight is provided to develop a clear policy and good practice for IT controls—enterprisewide. COBIT's *Management Guidelines* are composed of maturity models, to help determine the stages and expectation levels of control and compare them against industry norms; critical success factors, to identify the most important actions for achieving control over the IT processes; key goal indicators, to define target levels of performance; and key performance indicators, to measure whether an IT control process is meeting its objective.

## MONITORING: MEASURING AND COMPARING OUTCOMES FOR IMPROVEMENTS

Monitoring is fundamental to the extended enterprise governance model —part of management's stewardship responsibility is to make certain that what was originally agreed to be performed is being done and that it should be performed. Monitoring is needed to make sure that those to whom responsibility has been delegated are acting correctly and are being held accountable. It identifies the management actions required to get performance back to levels required by providing corrective direction. Monitoring of business activities requires organizational criteria and ensuring the achievement of performance objectives for the business activities. Monitoring is enabled by the definition of relevant performance indicators, the systematic and timely reporting of performance, and prompt action upon deviations.

The monitoring process for performance management is shown in Exhibit 3.3. In this architecture, the governance process starts with vision, mission, and values and provides direction to the organization. Goals, objectives, and expectations are set through strategic planning and translated into activities that will ensure reaching the goal through the effective use of operational planning.

Setting objectives can be viewed from three different planning perspectives:

1. Strategic

2. Long-range

3. Operational

Strategic planning includes planning the direction the enterprise and all its components will take going forward. It addresses the mission of the enterprise in terms of its main business. Outputs of strategic planning should include clear strategies for selecting business areas or market participation. Long-range planning analyzes alternatives to strategic options leading to the mission being achieved. Operational plans, however, are the day-to-day action plans addressing how specific timeline and measurable targets will be met. These action plans take into account assumptions for the periods, changes that need to be made, timetables, budget allocations, and individual responsibilities.

**Exhibit 3.3   Monitoring Process**

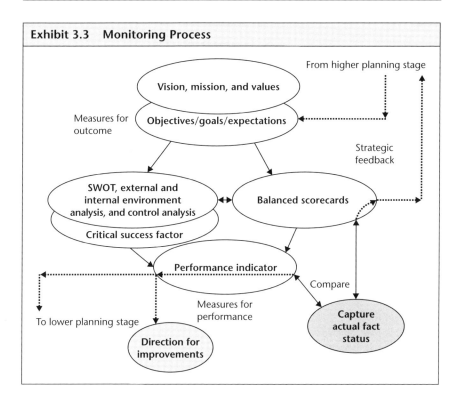

The process of utilizing the *SWOT (strength, weakness, opportunities, and threat) approach* may include an internal analysis of strengths and weaknesses of the organization and an external analysis at the main points in the environmental analysis, as well as the relationship between the two. It may also identify those points that pose threats or obstacles to performance and opportunities for the organization. CSFs (critical success factors) identify the most critical processes/resources needed to accomplish the goals. If an external opportunity exists, there must be an organizational ability to take advantage of that opportunity. For a further discussion on SWOT, as well as balanced scorecards, refer to Appendix B, "Performance Reference Model."

## ONGOING STRATEGY PROCESS: OPERATIONAL PERFORMANCE MONITORING

An enterprise needs to integrate management control with strategic learning to ensure that its strategies are adapting to meet the rapidly changing environment. Kaplan and Norton in the article "Double-Loop Management: Making Strategy a Continuous Process"[4] indicated that

"The balanced scorecard offers a solution: a double-loop process that integrates tactics management (management control) with strategy management (strategy learning). This new management system introduces two feedback loops that allow organizations to monitor and test strategy, to update their scorecard measures as needed and in turn, to adapt their strategies to changing environment."

With this looped management system, the strategy-learning loop/on-going strategy is the process whereby the executive team tests whether their strategy is working as planned and whether recent experience warrants any modifications. This loop provides an entities' scorecard to clarify and translate the vision and strategy, communicate and link related parties within the extended enterprise. The balanced scorecards goals should be developed in two phases:

1. The creation of value consistent with the mission is the overarching purpose of the entity

2. Strategy defining the unique organizational approach towards creating value

The actual results achieved should be compared with targets set, and any realized variances should be analyzed. The overall impact of external environmental condition changes, discontinuity of success factors, necessity of emergent strategy, and so on, should be considered. Business testing, learning, and adapting strategies are addressed during this process. Information and knowledge related to the area of continuous innovation may have significant added value and should be monitored. Strategy feedback from the management control loop also should be considered. The type of information that will usually drive innovation is significantly different from what a manager creates and relies on to run operations. It is broader in scope, softer in content, and exploratory in its acquisition process. This loop process, performed annually or in six-month periods, would be considered continuous monitoring. Strategy should be updated by testing hypothesis as replacement, improvement of current systems/resources, and/or implementation of a new products/services program.

The management control loop is where the balanced scorecard itself becomes the agenda for a periodic management meeting of the extended enterprise. Traditionally, the meeting is used to discuss the variance of actual and budget, and management explains why results fell short of targets and planned corrective actions. In the extended enterprise environment, this information is kept in a knowledge portal of the extended enterprise for knowledge sharing of tangible resource status, and the periodic face-to-face management meeting should focus on the balanced scorecard and report and discuss all strategically relevant measures, as well as performance-improving initiatives. It intensifies the focus on the strategy and identifies the management and organizational actions required to get performance back on track. The balanced scorecards are mainly used for planning and target setting and for strategic feedback and learning.

An example of this was reported by Dr. Steve Kirn, vice president of innovation and organizational development at Sears, a chain department store in the United States. In 1992, Sears was facing challenges on several fronts. The new CEO, Arthur Martinez, took over the helm at Sears and made a number of dramatic changes to reshape and rejuvenate the company. The first step the executive team set forth was to identify the key strategies. Defining world-class performance objectives was the team's next challenge by involving their large customers. The next challenge was focusing on the relationships among the major dimensions of the business, which enabled Sears to identify some counterintuitive findings and leverage feedback, creating a learning culture. As a result, the chain introduced a new strategy refocusing on operational excellence/efficient services, excellent selection and quality merchandise and partner relationships. Its scorecard was also updated to reflect this shift. The chain introduced an innovative strategy, tested it in real time, learned what was not working, and modified the strategy accordingly.[5]

The double-loop strategic management concept is a system that, when used, enables management teams to perform these critical functions:

- Monitor performance against the strategy
- Work as teams to interpret the data
- Develop new strategic insights
- Update the measures on scorecards
- Adapt their strategies to changing environments

By enabling dynamic adjustments to change—internally as well as externally—an extended enterprise can make strategy a continuous process.

## SUMMARY

Extended enterprises need to create value, or there is no purpose in either creating them or keeping them alive. Since the partners of the extended enterprise have other interests to pay homage to, namely their own board and stockholders, the vision and mission of the extended enterprise needs to be not only powerful but also crystal clear. It cannot get lost in the shuffle between the partners. Of course just as vital, the strategy needs to be constantly monitored for key performance, and adjustments should be made. It is to this end that various, well-accepted frameworks and performance models for use have been provided. All parties of the extended enterprise need to be assured that they are evaluating and monitoring the performance of the entity by the same approach.

## NOTES

1. *A Guide to Project Management Body of Knowledge,* the PMBOK guide (Project Management Institute, 2002), defines project management as the application of knowledge, skills, tools, and techniques to project activities to meet project requirements. Project management is accomplished through the use of processes such as initiating, planning, executing, controlling, and closing.
2. Robert S. Kaplan and David P. Norton, *The Balanced Scorecard: Translating Strategy Into Action* (Boston, MA: Harvard Business Review Press, 1996).
3. *Control Objectives for Information and Related Technology (COBIT) Framework* (Rolling Meadows, IL: IT Governance Institute, 2000).
4. Robert S. Kaplan and David P. Norton, "Double-Loop Management: Making Strategy a Continuous Process," *Harvard Business Review.*
5. Steve Kirn, "The Balanced Scorecard at Sears: A Compelling Place for Feedback and Learning," *Harvard Business Review,* vol. 2, no. 4 (July–August 2000).

# 4

# OPERATIONAL BUSINESS ACTIVITIES: VALUE REALIZATION FOR THE EXTENDED ENTERPRISE

## VALUE REALIZATION

The traditional business environment concentrated power in top management. However, in recent years many successful corporations have implemented radical changes in governance systems. Executives around the world are focusing on the orderly distribution of power and authority in the service of developing more competitive and responsible enterprises. The founding CEO of Visa International, Dee Hock, said, "The function of the 'CORE' (central management) is to enable its constituent parts."[1] He suggests that organizations distribute power and function to the maximum degree and seek infinite durability and diversity. Such ideas were not only once considered radical but have proven practical, at least for some organizations. Shell Oil Company established internal boards back in the mid-1990s to delegate decision making, including capital investment decisions, to three newly formed business units: upstream operations (explorations and productions), downstream operations (distribution, marketing, and sales), and chemicals and services (primarily information technology). This provided dramatic increases during the next four years in profits, growth, and in the introduction of innovative processes that directly impacted strategy.

Managers have generally thought and acted locally. Many times, they failed to ask the question: How do we service our overall vision and our compartmentalized missions? Over the last decade, the global/ local unit has been promulgated. In these fast-growing and diverse markets, each market has its own environment and requirements. This includes business partners/competitors, distribution channels, and pricing and resource availability. It would be difficult to manage such an environment from one location. Managers need to think and act globally, regionally, and locally, and must be sensitive to what is outside their normal purview. Trends in one location are just as important as those in another location. Innovations can be originated from both corporate and business units/subsidiaries. Both corporate innovation and business unit innovation can and should be shared globally. Value is only realized if the global and local innovation is captured and used to develop universally acceptable products and services through operational business activities. Value/benefits from operational activities includes higher revenue and profits, lower labor costs, and more efficient use of resources to enhance overall productivity.

In the extended enterprise, management must also capture innovation with outside partners at the global and local levels, share the innovation throughout the enterprise, and use this information in the further development of world-class products and services. This global sharing of information and knowledge is critical and difficult in any enterprise and becomes more critical and difficult in the extended enterprise. The organizational environment in the extended enterprise must resemble a network of distributed intelligence and the enterprise's business strategies must include multiple perspectives, customs, and business environments. There are two major challenges in the extended enterprises:

1. Consensus building
2. Managerial transformation

## Consensus Building

In a rapidly evolving competitive environment, it is natural that stakeholders in an enterprise start with different opinions on direction, priorities, and timing of actions. Consensus building among stakeholders becomes a critical element of enterprise management. However, consensus building across cultures, geographic locations, business units, and even among various partners is complex. To ensure effective consensus building, the following areas need to be considered:

- Debates must focus on interpretation of data, rather than disagreement, and top management must set the tone.

- Debates should be designed to reach consensus and arrive at actionable decisions.

- Information and knowledge must be shared and viewed as an enterprise resource and not used as a source of private power.

- Financial and human resource use must be planned within an unpredictable economic and regulatory environment. No one can fully predict the implications of discontinuities. One entity might start from its base of experience and move forward. Multiple migration paths in an evolving industry are also legitimate. Strategy in this evolving environment involves the customer's interest or preference and then reshapes the future using the coevolving and patching approaches as discussed in Chapter 2. The goal is to create new competitive advantages. At the same time, current businesses cannot be ignored since discontinuities do not happen overnight.

- The pace of change in today's competitive environment is accelerating. Although discontinuities within established organizations may not be obvious, enterprise governance implications of discontinuous change are even less so. Management needs to be more proactive to the change around them and their enterprises.

## Managerial Transformation

Transformation is not just about reducing costs, improving profitability, or reengineering. Instead, it is about the invention and implementation of new strategies and management processes. New ideas and a new understanding must drive the transformation. It must involve the entire organization, with top management leading the transformation effort. Top management needs to change the external perspective of the entire organization, as well as the internal perception of the entities' opportunities. Only a new and shared perception of the firm's opportunities can lead to new ways to compete. In addition, transformation must deal with tacit values and beliefs. This may have great influence on how managers act and respond. It also requires building new skill sets within the enterprise that include new markets, businesses, and approaches to creating and sustaining a competitive advantage at all levels. Finally, the transformation must be supported by new management processes, performance evaluation, and logistics. Above all, the transformation needs to be accepted and owned by the people responsible for its implementation on the ground.

As discussed in Chapter 3, double-loop management for making strategy a continuous process with a knowledge portal will help these challenges. However, a more integrated picture should be prepared for consensus building among the partners within an extended enterprise. This guideline suggests a blueprint to guide the transformation process. Managers must have a clear understanding of the elements of the transformation efforts. If they cannot see and understand the future, they cannot create value or innovation, let alone accept and own the transformation process.

## BLUEPRINT FOR KNOWLEDGE SHARING IN AN EXTENDED ENTERPRISE

Exhibit 4.1 shows a blueprint for providing information and sharing knowledge among individuals. It focuses on consensus building to assist readers in realizing the value of an extended enterprise. The exhibit shows a process that is run by human resources and/or machines (other resources) divided into operational business activities and information sharing activities. Operational business activities directly handle tangible resources based on information/order/origination provided by the

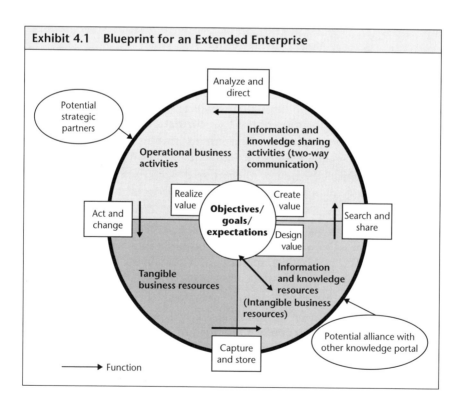

**Exhibit 4.1    Blueprint for an Extended Enterprise**

information sharing activities. The results of operational business activities, as well as objectives, goals, and expectations, are recorded as information/ intangible business resources and shared activities. The process continues in a counter-clockwise rotation, as shown by the direction of the arrows (functions) in Exhibit 4.1.

Solving how each participating stakeholder, each having different business processes/operational business activities and information systems/information sharing activities, can operate effectively in an extended enterprise environment is critical. The participants should at least share broad business objectives to provide world-class products and services to their customers/consumers. In particular, information-sharing activities (two-way communication) among partners of the extended enterprise are a key factor in achieving effective governance.

This blueprint can also be applied to an enterprise without extended activities for good practices. It is also noteworthy to stress that all current customers, partners, and suppliers are accounted for within the scope of the blueprint. Thus, only potential strategic partners and potential alliances with other knowledge portals are illustrated outside of the scope. Exhibit 4.2 illustrates the various relationships with a knowledge portal for an extended enterprise and information and knowledge resources

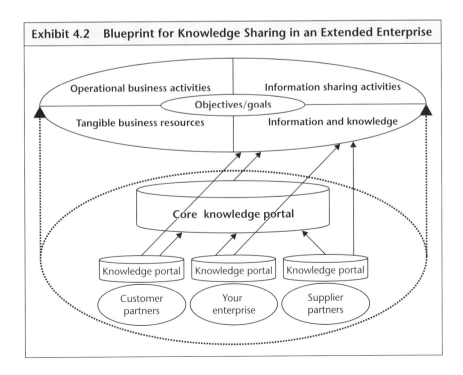

**Exhibit 4.2    Blueprint for Knowledge Sharing in an Extended Enterprise**

of the blueprint for knowledge sharing in an extended enterprise, as shown in Exhibit 4.1. A core knowledge portal should be available for all stakeholders. Also for each enterprise, a knowledge portal is provided for compartmentalization of knowledge activities. See Appendix F for additional discussion on knowledge portal.

## OBJECTIVES, GOALS, AND EXPECTATIONS

As shown in Exhibit 4.1, the most important components of the blueprint for extended enterprises are the objectives, goals, and expectations for the enterprise. The mission must be translated to goals and objectives so that the actions and decisions of the individuals are aligned and supportive of the entire organization. All decisions can then be based on how an action forwards the organization's vision. The vision, mission, and values of the extended enterprise form a continuum, or whole organization.

The contents of these components serve as the drivers of all business activities. They are used as criteria to measure and monitor these activities. Alternatively, expectations explain the behavior in terms of an individual's goals and what is expected in achieving these goals. Proactive participation and buy-in of the stakeholders are critical success factors for extended enterprise governance and control. The strategy learning loop should provide a clear definition of the contents and relationships and sharing of these contexts (data and relationships) among the partners/individuals through a core knowledge portal.

Also, for empowerment, compartmentalization of missions and visions for each partner and line management help in the management of the extended enterprise. A knowledge portal is provided for this purpose. Coaching as well as face-to-face meetings are the most effective communication tools for goal sharing and the knowledge portal supports the most effective and efficient usage of knowledge sharing.

## INFORMATION AND KNOWLEDGE RESOURCES (INTANGIBLE BUSINESS RESOURCES)

In Exhibits 4.1 and 4.2, the objectives, goals, and expectations are stored as information resources for goals sharing and buy-in participation of partners during information and knowledge sharing activities. Also, data that capture the status of critical tangible resources for decision making at each partner location through their operational activities are input, processed, and transferred to an information and knowledge depository and stored as information. This information will be compared with the objectives, goals, and expectations for performance monitoring during information and knowledge sharing activities.

In the extended enterprise environment, implementing competitive enterprise information resources for transparency of each partner's activities and sharing the status of their business among partners is one of the most important critical success factors for sound decision making and overall enlightened customer service. This information normally presents and clarifies the current status (content and relationship) of each part of the enterprise operation's critical tangible resources. In the context of today's global economy, information that captured the status of those critical tangible resources should be considered as a vital intangible resource requiring two-way communication among the stakeholders (especially partners) in the extended enterprise for sound decision making. Information can be represented as related data elements or as ideas that have been organized or shaped in some way for human understanding. Information, in a more fundamental component than knowledge and its use, provides a new perspective for interpreting events or shedding light on expected connections. In the context of today's global economy, information is a necessary commodity. Just exactly how it is used in various ways is most often described as knowledge. Knowledge is a dynamic human process using information to achieve outcomes. Relationships between *explicit knowledge* (that which is codified) and *implicit knowledge* (other knowledge contained within the human brain) involve knowledge management. Knowledge management in the enterprise context focuses on achieving the overall objectives of the enterprise. These can be classified into the following four domains within the enterprise's knowledge base:

1. *Goal relationships* include R&D and product design or product development, which flows to products or services. The goal relationships knowledge base includes the following:

    - *Goal base* refers to mission/domain, strategy plan, tactical plan, management goals, and operational level orders/origination. Sharing the objectives, goals, and expectations of each enterprise among the partners is critical for successful operation of extended enterprises in providing world-class quality products and services to customers. Goal relationships normally cover vision/ mission, domain, customer expectation, strategy, tactical and management plans, orders/origination, external situation, internal situation, critical success factors, product/services, and so on. R&D and product design or product development to flow of products or services is one of the critical relationships.

- *Monitoring base* refers to the ability of an extended enterprise-enabled organization to take action on information/data. It begins with putting the data into context, representing not only the status of the real world of the extended enterprise and what actions are possible given that status, but also what actions ought to be taken. The information on the status of the internal real world of the extended enterprise is normally gathered from business activity information and from the external real world of knowledge management activity information. The information for what action ought to be taken is often imported from planning activity information. The information for what actions are possible may be gathered from the knowledge base.

2. *Core business relationships* are the business activity systems, of each partner, that should generate information to identify the status of contents and relationships (contexts) of the following:

- Product/services
- Core business cash flow (accounts receivable and payable)
- Customer/suppliers
- Orders/generations/transactions among partners/alliances

3. *Resource relationships* identify the status of the enterprise's resources, which are used to support the core business activities and information and knowledge sharing activities. Three key resources have been identified to provide overall support:

- Human/partners
- Financial
- Others assets/environment, including information systems

4. *Knowledge relationships and knowledge-based management* is the most sophisticated domain in the extended enterprise system. Although the system itself has some decision-making capability programmed into it, the system also acts as an extension of the human ability to store and process knowledge. Sometimes this

can transform data into knowledge through complex statistical and simulation analysis. But in most cases, they are facts of customers, products, resources, best practices, benchmarks, and so on. External environment information should be carefully captured and stored for sound ongoing strategy activities.

How to share information and goals among several diverse constituents requires a great deal of care and sophistication. Information coordination requirements are numerous, including strategic objectives, capacity constraints, as well as logistics, manufacturing, and procurement requirements for all partners. Information repositories (knowledge portal) need to be carefully designed and implemented to meet this coordination requirement.

## INFORMATION SHARING ACTIVITIES
## (TWO-WAY COMMUNICATION)

The success of ongoing consensus building within the enterprise depends on how well management communicates with all stakeholders in building a common culture, and in common acceptance and ownership of its mission and strategy. This needs to be complemented by ready accessibility to the underlying knowledge base so that it can be effectively searched and shared internally, and, most importantly, to the extent required externally. Current Net-centric technologies, such as groupware and the Internet, provide the technology platform to support this enhanced level of communication. However, human action in response to action plans derived from clear strategics, based on using this infrastructure, is required for communication to be effective and trusted.

During the formation stage of an extended enterprise, the knowledge base of partners is embodied in their initial productive capabilities and in their service offerings. After the initial set-up period, knowledge creation and dissemination are likely to become the principle means of growth of the enterprise. The ability to embody and embed knowledge and learning must be at the heart of every extended enterprise strategy.

Effective information-sharing activities for consensus building are sometimes referred to as two-way communication. Achievement of common understanding, common ownership, and common acceptance are also required. Sound decision making, based on the analysis of this knowledge base and information, will help establish the requisite strategic directions to achieve value creation.

## OPERATIONAL BUSINESS ACTIVITIES

Information sharing activities generate actions, directions, orders, and origination affecting operational business activities. Operational business activities frequently involve the use of the following tangible resources:

- Core business activities relating to the flow of products and/or services. These may encompass purchasing, production, marketing, and distribution activities, for example.

- Core business cash-flow components. These might include payments to suppliers and collection from the customers.

- Provision of support that is necessary for the core business. This might include deployment and optimal use of human, financial, and other resources.

- Planning, acquisition, and allocation of the resources for activities related to provision of support.

## TANGIBLE BUSINESS RESOURCES

Operational business activities can change the status of tangible resources, such as products, facilities, people, and capital. The status of external resources, such as customers, vendors, and investors can also be changed by these directions. The status of these changes is captured as information and stored. These changes in status provide fresh information as a base for reflecting continuous innovative goal activities expressed as objectives, goals, and expectations for effective enterprise management.

## VALUE CREATION CYCLE

*Value* is designed and created by a continuous innovation process matching the strategic objectives, goals, and expectations of the enterprise. Performance management creates value by providing knowledge and sharing information for management to set objectives and compare actual performance against these objectives. Corrective actions (based on monitoring) can be initiated. The strategy setting and subordinate action plans governing operational activities are derived after the analysis of information/knowledge and decision making in information-sharing activities. An organization's future success depends on its people's knowledge, skill, creativity, and motivation. A sound governance structure should be implemented to provide an environment that meets these conditions and realizes the values. Attitudes and motivation are highly influenced by these factors:

- Visionary goals and incentives
- Self-confidence of work and accomplishment
- Favorable working environment and enterprise culture
- Future of the organization
- Encouragement and support for innovation/changes

In the extended environment, leadership plays a critical role for implementing these value cycles. A project officer should be assigned for the governance role of an extended enterprise project. Senior management and team leaders must create, develop, and express visions and goals. They must make people see that it is everyone's job to create ideas, and they must create an environment in which ideas are challenged with respect, information is shared, and management is conducted openly. They must insist on positive outcomes for both short-term goals and long-term vision, and they must involve staff fully in achieving the ultimate objective—otherwise, people will again begin to look inwardly. Further, taking charge of a project might not be in itself entrepreneurial, but one still needs to identify and express the objective, and form and activate an effective team. Senior management and team leaders must also realistically assess the organization's strengths and weaknesses, identify changes needed, include changing corporate culture through individuals, not vice versa, strive to satisfy the needs of both employees and customers, cherish customers and their input, and use objective measures of customer response.

## SUMMARY

With managers having traditionally thought and acted locally first by nature, it is indeed a challenge to participate in the extended enterprise, where innovation must be captured and shared at the global level as well as local. This paradigm shift occurs regardless of how business was conducted in the past. Consensus building, a great skill to have for any manager, is an absolute requirement for participation in the extended environment. Enterprises are forced into relationships where cultures will clash, even within the same national boundaries. The chapter offered a suggested blueprint for conducting business with partners, utilizing a focus on operational business activities and information sharing activities.

It is through these two steps that the value is both created and realized. The advent of IT solutions, such as groupware and e-mail, has allowed the focus of two-way communication and sharing to become a knowledge base for others in the enterprise. If the objectives, goals, and expectations are shared by the partners, and monitored in a real time basis, there is a much greater chance for the overall enterprise objectives to be achieved. In the end, that is what every executive and every enterprise is driving to achieve.

## NOTE

1. Dee Hock, *Birth of the Chaordic Age* (San Francisco: Berrett-Koehler, 1999).

# 5

# GOVERNANCE FRAMEWORK
# FOR THE EXTENDED ENTERPRISE

## GOVERNANCE DEFINITION

*Governance* can be defined as the exercise of ethical corporate behavior by directors or others in the wealth-creation process, as part of how they provide stewardship over the business of the entity. In the current legal structure of private sector entities, boards of directors normally have primary responsibility for the governance of an organization. The critical point for the boards is defining under what conditions the board should get involved with major decisions normally made by the entity's management. The big challenge for boards is to walk the fine line between governing the organization in the interest of shareholders on one side, and actually shadow-managing the business on the other. As a minimum, boards should evaluate whether their CEO is building the organization's franchise (market, people, and capabilities) and delivering long-term financial results coupled with entity sustainability. The degree to which the board demonstrates its independence and accountability from the CEO in the shareholders' perspective has given rise to significant concerns for governance in many entities around the world. This topic has certainly gained renewed prominence in many enterprises worldwide as they attempt to deal with current market conditions. No one need look any further than the reform law of the Sarbanes-Oxley Act, signed into legislation in July 2002 in the United States. This is quite simply one of the most far-reaching laws on corporate governance in the last seven decades. Of course, the issue of governance has some long-standing definitions.

The Organization for Economic Co-operation and Development (OECD) defines corporate governance as a set of relationships between an organization's management, board of directors, shareholders, and stakeholders. Good corporate governance should provide proper incentives for the board of directors and management to pursue objectives that are in the interests of the organization and stakeholders. Corporate governance initiatives should focus on the problems that result from the separation of ownership and control and should be directed at obtaining effective monitoring, thereby encouraging more effective use of resources by entity management.

The Bank for International Settlements (BIS) defined the governance arrangements in *Enhancing Corporate Governance in Banking Organizations*[1] as encompassing the set of relationships between the entity's management and its governing body, its owners, and its other stakeholders and providing the structure through which three objectives are met:

1. The entity's overall objectives are set.
2. The method of attaining those objectives is outlined.
3. The manner in which performance will be monitored is described.

The International Federation of Accountants (IFAC) set out its view that the auditor's responsibility in governance is to obtain an understanding of the entity and its environment, and to discuss matters of governance interest with those responsible for governance in the entity. Auditors do this by examining the structure, mandate, and processes of the governance function and the responsibility, experience, overall attitude, philosophy, and operating style of those charged with governance.

The Sarbanes-Oxley Act of 2002 demonstrated a firm resolve by the U.S. Congress to improve corporate responsibility. The act was created to restore investor confidence in U.S. public markets, which was damaged by business scandals and lapses in corporate governance. Although the act and supporting regulations have rewritten the rules for accountability, disclosure, and reporting, the act's many pages of legalese support a simple premise: good corporate governance and ethical business practices are no longer optional niceties.[2] It introduced stringent new rules with the stated objective: "to protect investors by improving the accuracy and reliability of corporate disclosures made pursuant to the securities laws."

It also introduced a number of deadlines, the prime ones being:

- Companies specified by the Act are required to meet the financial reporting and certification mandates for any end of year financial statements filed after November 2004.

- Smaller companies and foreign companies must meet these mandates for any statements filed after April 15, 2005.

The act, named after its main architects, Senator Paul Sarbanes and Representative Michael Oxley, followed a series of very high-profile lapses of integrity, such as Enron and WorldCom. Sarbanes-Oxley itself is organized into 11 main sections, although subsections 302, corporate responsibility for financial reports; 401, disclosures in periodic reports; 404, management assessment of internal controls; 409, real-time issuer disclosures; 802, criminal penalties for altering documents; and 906, corporate responsibility for financial reports, are currently some of the most significant subsections dealing with financial reporting.

In an effort to draw focus to the critical importance of governance, the IT Governance Institute has issued a governance model, as shown in Exhibit 5.1, providing the structure and practices for an enterprise to do the following:

- Set and put into motion objectives, goals, and expectations (plan and organize).

- Determine a means of attaining those objectives through enterprise activities and utilization of the enterprise's resources (acquire, implement, deliver, and support).

**Exhibit 5.1    Governance Model**

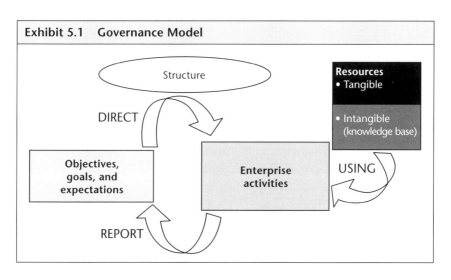

- Establish and control a set of comprehensive monitoring and reporting performance guidelines (monitor and control).
- Implement a well-organized structure and adequate accountabilities for effective governance.

This governance is the responsibility of the board of directors. The directors exercise that responsibility by providing leadership and by ensuring that all resources, including information technology, sustain and extend the organization's strategies and objectives. Good governance provides proper incentives for each of the stakeholders to pursue the objectives that are in the interests of both the organization and the stakeholders and it facilitates effective monitoring. Furthermore, good governance should encourage stakeholders within the entity to continually look for ways to use resources more efficiently.

Resources can typically be separated into two groups, tangible and intangible. The group that has typically received the lion's share of attention, *tangible resources,* such as property, buildings and equipment, financial and similar resources, need to be planned and organized, acquired, and implemented, delivered and supported, and monitored and controlled—for the dual purposes of realizing benefits and managing risks. However, the second group of resources, those that are *intangible* in nature, such as patents, copyrights, and other organizational useful information/knowledge, also should be governed in a similar way.

In organizations today, components of a formal governance mechanism include boards of directors, management structures, reward and recognition policies, entity procedures, delegated authority levels, and more. Such formal mechanisms define who has the power to make particular types of decisions. However, the guidance issued by international bodies, such as the OECD, BIS, IFAC, and ITGI referred to earlier, do not yet provide an appropriately comprehensive governance framework for the extended enterprise, nor are the value of intangible resources properly recognized. Therefore, there is a real need to have a revised framework for governance that can be adapted to include what is meant by the extended enterprise environment.

## ENTERPRISE GOVERNANCE CHALLENGE IN THE EXTENDED ENTERPRISE

The nature of the technology environment today enables the speedy and effective construction and testing of products, scalability to new and larger markets, and efficient partnering with outside entities as never before possible. An extended enterprise that expects to be competitive must develop and nurture these organizational capabilities to match this expanding environment. The development of an entity's capacity for rapid organization prototyping is viewed as both a reaction to, as well as a driver of, growth, innovation, and value creation. Without such a capacity for rapid prototyping, the enterprise will not adequately meet the constantly changing demands for excellence in performance, people, management, and leadership. The generally accepted model of an enterprise must be able to evolve to new organizational forms to accommodate and respond to emerging external factors. However, continually redesigning the organization with implementation within short time frames stresses its capacity to effectively and efficiently manage the changing roles and responsibilities. Whenever possible, entities should consider the utilization of world leading partners or alliances, as well as their available resources, to accomplish the needed redesign of the organization and resource structure where a quantum change is considered necessary.

The traditional organization often has controlled boundaries that tell people what they can and cannot do, like barbed wire keeping people under control. These are also known as central command-and-control structured organizations, where all decisions are made in one central area. However, in an extended enterprise environment, these boundaries should be elastic, stretching to fit the environment and allowing the degree of autonomy necessary for innovation and flexibility when working with partners. This view is described as a "core" approach to management. Its focus is on quick action, sharing and leveraging on the strengths of others for the accomplishment of enterprise goals. Therefore, managers need to view boundaries as rubber bands, with high elasticity and extensive flexibility. The many varied demands imposed on the entity when operating in this extended environment, and the multiple and different demands brought on by the various partners, suggest the need for a clear and concise governance framework. This framework could then be adapted and used by all entities that either are in, or are looking to participate in, an extended enterprise environment. Certainly, once an approach such as this is adopted, there still is the need to exert strong performance measurement to determine if the partnering arrangement is meeting the needs of the core organization.

The globally competitive landscape poses a challenge for the application of governance concepts in the extended enterprise. The business world today is gripped by tremendous cross-currents concerning the philosophy, approach, and practice of governance. Scandals and other high profile disorders have their effects on a governance approach as well. While many industrial corporations have traditionally concentrated power in their CEOs and top management, some of the most success-ful corporations in recent years have begun to implement a new gover-nance framework, focusing on the "core" of the enterprise. This new governance framework is continuously evolving and emerging. CEOs who are running entities that are involved in extended enterprise are gradually redefining their basic relationship with the board and treating directors as equal partners. Some board members of corporations, in addition to engaging in thorough examination of an entity's structure and operation, have begun to redefine their stakeholder-based relation-ships. They recognize that a successful board will bring coherence to the system. This clarity will allow diverse stakeholders in the extended enter-prise—shareholders, employees, government, competitors, and partners—not only to cope with each other's independent perspectives but also to benefit from them as well.[3]

One such example of the *core* approach involves an organization in the automotive industry. As early as 1995, the Chrysler Corporation's board started holding face-to-face meetings with many of its major insti-tutional shareholders as part of its comprehensive corporate governance policies review process. In its 1996 Proxy Statement, Chrysler reported that an outside independent member of the board had also attended each of the institutional shareholder's face-to-face meetings, and had exchanged candid views and opinions with representatives in attendance. Further, Chrysler's board developed a specific mission statement cover-ing corporate governance of their extended enterprises for evaluation of existing business structures as well as processes and guidance for future changes. By every measure in existence, this approach is most certainly a performance measurement approach that led Chrysler to quickly understand and capitalize on learning points of their partners.

In essence, Chrysler's board plays an active role in defining and attaining the organization's mission and functions as an independent partner in major strategic decision-making processes. Their corporate and extended enterprise missions, visions, values, goals, and strategies are shared with the business units throughout the enterprise and busi-ness partners (suppliers, customers, etc.) at all worldwide locations. Each business unit and business partner develops explicit vision and strategy, formulates strategic aims, measures specific goals and action plans, allocates resources and sets targets, follows up on results in learn-ing, and reexamines the vision.

Another example involves a major air carrier. It took what was con-sidered at the time to be a radical step and sold a majority of its stocks to its employees and effectively connected them to the governance of the company by restructuring the representation of the board. Its 12-member board included three employee directors selected by the unions and salaried management employees, four independent directors selected by previous independent directors, and five public directors elected by the public shareholders. Such a governance structure requires all stakeholders to balance their interests and to take into account demands and constraints. In such an approach to governance, employees, managers, directors, and shareholders must recognize and understand their role and its overall impact on independence. They also need to align their various agendas for the good of the enterprise. That approach to governing is still unique, and has caused the airline a tremendous amount of uncertainty and doubt. So, the approach must be weighed with the environment, and its ability to get all the partners working together for a common goal. It should be noted that these types of approaches, giving a wide representation of stakeholder interest, are more prevalent in a traditional German economic system than in the United States.

## GOVERNANCE STRUCTURE FOR THE EXTENDED ENTERPRISE

In the extended enterprise environment, there is no standard preexisting governance structure such as a board of directors. Each separate enterprise of course has its own board. Sometimes, all that exists is a service level agreement. The issue of governance is much broader than that commonly appreciated and understood. It commonly has three facets:

1. Governance of each corporation by its separate board of directors
2. Governance of intercorporate entities
3. Governance of intracorporate entities

The process of planning and setting up an extended enterprise governance center will no doubt only place a high cost on the organization without adding value in a diversified and a wide-ranging business environment. A new governance core structure, which creates value but not sheer overhead, should be implemented. (See Appendix C for a detailed discussion on core versus central approach.) It should be global whenever possible. Furthermore, the form may consist of a global core knowledge management implementation using a knowledge portal. In the extended enterprise, a focus for both IT and people tracks and levels is extended to outside the organization. This includes business partners, suppliers, customers, and outsourcers. The needed implementation of a core information repository in an extended enterprise is complex work. However, to provide a clear picture, the complexities presented need to be resolved. Through the provision of a core repository of information—referred to as a core knowledge-portal and a logical Web-based approach—the real value of a portal can be experienced under a well-organized project plan. This practice represents a new form for a suggested governance structure for the extended enterprise. (For further detail on knowledge portal, see Appendix F.) This approach creates space for the business to act as an integrator and to help each component part or contributor of the extended enterprise to realize its full value potential, while not being overloaded with the details that can be involved with organizational bureaucracy. To put it another way, the traditional governance model usually adopts a passive guardianship role, while the transformed model plays an active role in the support of achieving the business imperatives.

The impact of the governance model in the extended enterprise will pervade all members of the organization starting from the board, through to all levels of employees throughout the enterprise. Additionally, as previously described, it will impact business partners, suppliers, and customers at all locations. Implementation of a core knowledge portal, described earlier, should be assigned to a specific program officer. That person would most likely also have the overall project governance responsibility.

The cube model presented in Exhibit 5.2 has three dimensions:

1. Enterprise activities, as defined by the Malcolm Baldrige National Quality Award:[4]

   - *Business processes* are those nonproduct/nonservice processes that are considered the most important to business growth and success by senior leaders. Among others, examples include research and development, technology acquisition, information and knowledge management, supply chain management, supplier and customer partnering, outsourcing, merger and acquisition, global expansion, project management and marketing.

   - *Support processes* are those that support daily operations and product and service delivery but are not usually designed in detail with the products and services. Examples are financial and accounting, facilities management, legal services, human resource services, public relations and other administrative services.

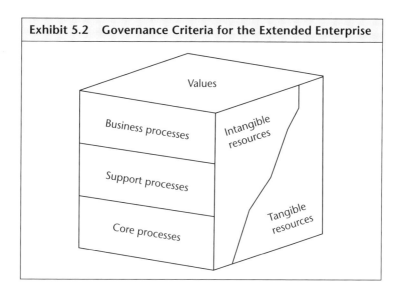

**Exhibit 5.2   Governance Criteria for the Extended Enterprise**

- *Core processes* are the enterprise's key products and service design and delivery processes, with the aim of improving its market place and operational performance.

2. Resources

- *Intangible resources* are useful information/knowledge bases. These are the most critical resources for extended enterprise governance because the governance structure heavily relies on a knowledge portal sharing among the partners. The reliance on intellectual resources on one enterprise owner is never enough; the senior management should orchestrate the dynamic combination of complementary skills and assets of the partners to generate and then realize innovative ideas and product improvements.

- *Tangible resources* are financial, human, facilities, and similar resources. Normally, complementary skills (intangible resources) are combined with these assets (tangible resources) to produce world-class products and services. Alliance with world-class resource partners should be considered to extend the scope of available tangible resources.

3. Objectives, goals, and expectations: values

- *Values* are the driver for objectives, goals, and expectations. Sharing the same goals among partners is a critical success factor of the governance of the extended enterprise. Goals/ objectives are set through strategic planning and translated into activities that will ensure reaching the goal through the effective use of operational planning.

## GOVERNANCE OBJECTIVES FOR THE EXTENDED ENTERPRISE

In addition to the three dimensions just briefly discussed, four inter-linked objectives need to be considered for inclusion when designing the governance structure for the extended enterprise. After each is described at a high level, Exhibit 5.3 shows the relationship between those objectives and the three dimensions described earlier.

The four interlinked objectives are as follows:

1. **Leadership.** The ability and process to translate vision into de-sired behaviors that are followed at all levels of the extended enter-prise. This is the driver of the value dimension of the governance cube presented in Exhibit 5.2 and actually implementing the values. The challenges for this governance objective are as follows:

   ▪ *Promoting leadership by reflective practitioners.* To be suc-cessful in the extended enterprise, the leadership must think and react looking ahead. This means there must be a con-tinual acquisition and renewal of knowledge, a willingness

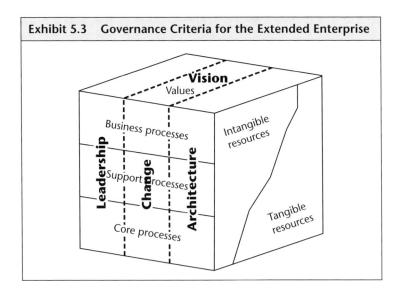

**Exhibit 5.3    Governance Criteria for the Extended Enterprise**

to learn and change and a willingness to do things differently. Initiating "outside-the-box" thinking is required to generate future growth and innovation. This can also be expressed as innovation or strategic leadership.

- *Educating managers, employees, business partners, suppliers, and perhaps customers on the applications of technology.* This will enable them to make decisions knowing the power and limitation of the technology. Senior leaders also should serve as a role model through their ethical behavior and their personal involvement in various activities such as planning, coaching, employee recognition, commitment, communication, public activities, development of future leaders, and review of performance. In short, this is empowerment.

- *Carrying out extended enterprise mapping (knowledge portal/knowledge base).* In this high-velocity environment of change, an enterprise's relationships can be so complex that they could be collaborating in one area and, at the same time, competing with the same partner, that is, airlines co-sharing alliance programs. Mapping of these relationships is crucial to understanding them and the dynamics of how they work. It also acts as a sourcing and disseminating marketmaker to ensure enterprisewide access to world-class, low-cost capabilities. The mapping provides a matrix for understanding confusing and diverse operations and relationships within the extended enterprise. It also serves to present and describe the value added to the organizations.

2. **Vision.** The clear definition of what the extended enterprise needs to implement to achieve the required change. This can be achieved by the value designing stage of the value cycle. The challenges for this governance criterion are:

- *Setting up and sustaining the knowledge, information, and technology infrastructure (knowledge portal/knowledge base).* Knowledge is a key component in both products and services as well as in the business processes supporting them. Thus, implementing the capabilities to embody and interleave knowledge and informational learning needs to be a driver of an enterprise's strategy. In the new extended enterprise, effective use of human capital is one of the key success factors for building competitive advantage. This is otherwise referred to as either knowledge sharing or as the creation of a knowledge portal (accessible knowledge store).

- *Establishing a driven, value-based enterprise.* Having clear vision and values are critical in the extended environment, where market conditions can be unstable and the number of opportunities is almost endless (the vision and values determine where the enterprise wishes to go). The directions, values, and expectations should help guide all activities and decisions of the extended enterprise.

- *Building an integrated and aligned strategy.* Enterprises need to establish a holistic organizational strategy, thus ensuring the strategy is aligned with the vision, the organizational systems, and with the demands of the external environment. Customer-driven quality and operational performance are additional key strategic issues. Provision of world-class products and services is the driver of customer satisfaction, customer retention, building new markets, and obtaining market share. Operational performance improvement contributes to both short-term and long-term productivity growth and cost/price competitiveness. This strategic impact is described as having customer focus or customer alignment as a major component.

3. **Change.** Should bring in a significant, measurable improvement in business performance. This should be achieved by the value creation stage of the value cycle. The challenges for attaining this governance objective are:

- *Effectively using a balanced scorecard performance management system (knowledge portal/knowledge base) designed for the business in question.* Monitoring in this format can have a crucial impact on driving business strategy and strategic outcome. It is important that balanced scorecard coverage extends to all enterprise strategies and to the whole of the enterprise business architecture.

- *Applying appropriate key measurement and monitoring criteria (CSF/KPI/KGI).* This will provide reportable governance over external partner relationships in the extended enterprise.

- *Making decisions within the enterprise needs to be based on having ready access to relevant data and information.* Close analysis is needed between goals and information elements in reaching the decision taken. The information used needs to provide sufficient, timely, and transparent data covering the status of key business resources and activities of all stakeholders within the extended enterprise. It will also be necessary to establish effective control procedures covering macroeconomic risks, business risks as well as a comprehensive risk management process so that monitoring performance is reliable and sustainable.

4. **Architecture.** The business concept used to describe the cohesive and integrated approach established to achieve the vision and desired results. To be able to utilize the architecture for the required results, the enterprise must work to provide some basic tenets that make up the architecture. The following are the most prevalent attributes:

- *Developing an innovative organizational structure (based on the knowledge portal/knowledge base).* To take advantage of the dynamics of the extended enterprise, entities need to take on the organizational forms, the language, and the cultural style that will support the development of a high-performance culture. This can also be referred to as setting up the proper enterprise architecture.

- *Implementing and evaluating speedily set-up organization prototypes to be able to shift to differing organizational forms to respond to external factors.* The number of uncertainties in the business environment, where the competitive landscape is continually changing, requires that entities operating in the extended enterprise environment must implement and evaluate the prospects of new prototypes for the future. The enterprise architecture also requires a complementary system architecture in a suitably integrated form for optimal autonomy and flexibility.

- *Providing sound information linkages and knowledge service flow for IT infrastructure partners within the extended enterprise.* A technology reference and IT management process guideline for the extended enterprise should be established to support the provision. IT governance is now the key for successful governance but it is also a needed approach that serves as the enabler for the new form of business model being proposed.

If the relationships of the aforementioned criteria, containing both dimensions of governance as well as the interlocked objectives, were to be shown with those of a typical governance structure, it might appear in a three-dimensional cube as depicted in Exhibit 5.3. To try and simplify the presentation, what this says is that the vision of an extended enterprise should be aligned with its values. Additionally, leadership, change, and architecture need to be interwoven with the various processes of that enterprise.

## COMPARISON WITH EXCELLENCE MODELS

The enterprise objectives can be readily extended in scope through matching them with business excellence models on quality management. There are a number of business quality excellence and performance management models that can be adapted to a governance measurement criteria; however, the four that are most commonly referred to are: the EFQM model for excellence in the European Union, the Deming Prize in Japan, ISO 9000-2000, which has global application, especially in the manufacturing environment and the Malcolm Baldrige quality framework in the United States.

Embedding performance measurement systems within the enterprise activities is important to hard-wire the changes made in support of business quality excellence, as well as to have the means to verify or test what has been achieved. Exhibit 5.4 presents at a high-level the four aforementioned models, and maps how they address each of the governance criteria for an extended enterprise.

The EFQM (European Framework for Quality Management) Excellence Model was established by the EFQM (European Foundation for Quality Management), a not-for-profit membership foundation based in Brussels. The European Commission endorses it. Similar to the Malcolm Baldrige Model in the United States and the Deming Prize in Japan, it is designed to improve services and products/manufacturing quality in organizations. Its mission is to stimulate and assist organizations throughout Europe to participate in improvement activities leading to excellence in customer satisfaction, employee satisfaction, and positive impact on society. The fundamental objective of the EFQM Excellence Model is to deliver outstanding results.

The Deming Prize was introduced in 1951 by the Japanese Union of Scientists and Engineers (JUSE) to honor W. Edwards Deming and drive the implementation of quality control. The Deming Prize provides a checklist for policies, organization, information, standardization, quality assurance, maintenance, improvement, effects, and future plans. It also provides a checklist for evaluating executive performance, which includes coverage of leadership understanding, policies on leadership approach,

**Exhibit 5.4 Comparison of Governance Criteria and Various Excellence Models**

| Governance Objectives for the Extended Enterprise | European Foundation for Quality Management | Deming Prize | International Organization for Standardization (ISO) 9000:2000 (Quality Management Systems) | Malcolm Baldrige National Quality Award |
|---|---|---|---|---|
| **Leadership** | ■ People development and involvement<br>■ Partnership development<br>■ Continuous learning, innovation, and improvement | ■ Policies<br>■ Organization<br>■ Human resources<br>■ Leadership, understanding | ■ Leadership<br>■ Environment and purpose | ■ Leadership<br>■ Organizational profile<br>■ Human resource focus |
| **Vision** | ■ Constancy of purpose<br>■ Customer focus | ■ Future plans/strategies | ■ Customer focus | ■ Strategic planning<br>■ Customer and market focus |
| **Performance Management** | ■ Results orientation<br>■ Public responsibility | ■ Maintenance and improvement<br>■ Effects<br>■ Quality assurance | ■ Continuous improvement<br>■ Supplier focus | ■ Business results |
| **Architecture** | ■ Management by processes and facts | ■ Standardization<br>■ Information | ■ Process approach<br>■ Systems approach | ■ Information and analysis<br>■ Process management |

organization for leadership deployment, human resources and implementation from a leadership deployment perspective.

ISO 9000:2000 standards are published by the International Standards Organization and are used for establishing a management system that provides confidence in the conformance of the product or service to an established set of specified requirements. There are five sections in the standard that specify activities that need to be considered when implementing a quality management system and four separating sections that deal with specific requirements. These include adequately addressing a quality management system, management responsibilities, performance management and measurement, and analysis and improvement.

The Malcolm Baldrige National Quality Award (MBNQA) was established by the U.S. Department of Commerce in 1987 to promote total quality management as an increasingly important approach to the competitiveness of American companies. The MBNQA has evolved from a quality focus to an award for performance excellence. It covers leadership, strategic planning, customer and market focus, information and analysis, human resource focus, process management, and business results (customer, financial and market, human resource, supplier and company specifics).

For further detail on each of these models, and the criteria that make up the models, see Appendix D.

## LEADERSHIP: DRIVER FOR VALUES AND GOVERNANCE IMPLEMENTATION

Among the key objectives for proper governance, leadership has been identified as the most vital, and is therefore considered a key success factor for implementing effective structures for the extended enterprise. Leaders normally create vision, drive change, and create the integrated architecture, linking all the objectives together. Leaders motivate others to work toward a common goal and need followers and disciples who buy into the vision, strategy, and values. Leaders also empower the creation of knowledge (processes and methods), and focus on delivering results.

Daniel Goleman describes six styles of leadership: [5]

1. Coercive leaders demand immediate compliance.

2. Authoritative leaders are able to mobilize people toward achieving a vision.

**3.** Affiliative leaders create emotional bonds and harmony.

**4.** Democratic leaders build consensus through participation.

**5.** Pacesetting leaders expect excellence and self-direction.

**6.** Coaching leaders develop people for the future.

The authoritative style has the strongest positive impact on the climate of a group. On the other end of the spectrum, the coercive style has the most negative impact on the climate of an extended enterprise, all other things being equal. In the extended environment, many times there are conflicting priorities, and a flexible leadership style is many times the most successful. Not all leaders will exhibit all the aforementioned styles, nor would that be a desired trait. However, the more styles a leader is able to exhibit to match different circumstances, the better for leadership of the enterprise. Leaders who have mastered four or more styles—especially the authoritative, democratic, affiliative, and coaching styles—typically achieve the very best climate and business performance.

In the dynamics of an extended environment, there is no room for leaders who motivate by fear or leaders who are autocratically self-important. Everything about this new model is driven by trust, teamwork, and shared beliefs. If this leadership style does not radiate from the top, then all the other work of putting the extended enterprise model in place will ultimately be futile. The governance of the extended enterprise is shared among the troops, yet for the model to even have a chance for success, it must be adopted and cultivated by the entity's CEOs.

## MATURITY LEVELS OF LEADERSHIP

Using the leadership styles described previously, an enterprise may wish to measure itself as to the effectiveness of its leadership capabilities, as well as its peers. Using this approach, an entity is better able to measure where it needs to be to meet the challenges of the extended enterprise activities. A suggested leadership maturity model proposed for building a successful extended enterprise is described in Exhibit 5.5.[6]

Having a level 5 leader at the top of an extended enterprise provides a hierarchy of capabilities, as well as being the prerequisite for transforming an organization from good to great. Each of the other four layers is appropriate in its own right, but none have the power of level 5. Level 5 requires the capabilities of all the lower levels, plus the special characteristics attributed to those at level 5.

| Exhibit 5.5  Maturity Levels of Leadership | | |
|---|---|---|
| *Level* | *Type* | *Description* |
| 1 | Highly capable individual | Makes productive contributions through talent, knowledge, skills, and good work habits |
| 2 | Contributing team member | Contributes to the achievement of group objectives; works effectively with others in group setting |
| 3 | Competent manager | Organizes people and resources toward the effective and efficient pursuit of predetermined objectives |
| 4 | Effective leader | Catalyzes commitment to and vigorous pursuit of a clear and compelling vision; stimulates the group to high performance standards |
| 5 | Level 5 executive | Builds enduring greatness through a paradoxical combination of personal humility plus professional will |

## MATURITY MODEL FOR EVALUATING THE LEVEL OF GOVERNANCE OF THE EXTENDED ENTERPRISE

The maturity model has been developed as a benchmark to evaluate the level of governance of the extended enterprise, as illustrated in Exhibit 5.6. The header of each column in Exhibit 5.6 is the knowledge or competency characteristic for each of the previously defined governance objectives:

- *Leadership.* Scope definition of the extended enterprise for alliance
- *Vision.* Core knowledge portal for best practices
- *Change.* Balanced scorecard for performance management
- *Architecture.* Enterprise architecture for IT governance

To use the maturity levels, using a scaling from 1 to 5 representing the most mature, the following general ranking might be used to present how an enterprise could be presented for *overall governance*.

*Level 1.* Each partner/party has its own knowledge base.

*Level 2.* Start sharing knowledge among partners.

*Level 3.* Define knowledge for sharing among partners.

*Level 4.* Apply shared knowledge is managed and measured within the extended enterprise.

*Level 5.* Use continuous improvements in knowledge sharing and implementation.

The second item normally covers the *strategic objectives* of the extended enterprise and provides maturity level as follows:

*Level 1.* Partial alliance is identified and initialized.

*Level 2.* Core activities identified in level 1 begin to be integrated.

*Level 3.* All activities defined as part of the extended enterprise are fully integrated.

*Level 4.* Monitoring activities associated with successful partnering are put into action.

*Level 5.* Activities associated with knowledge management are put into practice.

The third item mainly addresses *resources*, such as:

*Leadership.* Human resources/empowerment.

*Vision.* Customer.

*Change.* Core business resources.

*Architecture.* IT resources.

Maturity level could be generalized as:

*Level 1.* Initiate sharing.

*Level 2.* Normal sharing.

*Level 3.* Defined.

*Level 4.* Shared resources monitored.

*Level 5.* Knowledge management resources shared.

Those organizations able to achieve a level 5 in the maturity model truly will be able to share in the rewards that are only available to world-class enterprises. Practical and gradual implementation should be considered for formation of a competitive extended enterprise.

## TOOLS FOR THE GOVERNANCE OF THE EXTENDED ENTERPRISE

### Enterprise Index Model

When extended enterprises look to transform their governance system to one that is customer oriented and demonstrate world-class core competencies, they really should be looking to develop an enterprise index of

**Exhibit 5.6  Maturity Model for the Extended Enterprise**

| Level | Leadership | Vision | Change | Architecture |
|---|---|---|---|---|
| 1 | ■ The scope of the extended enterprise is not clear.<br>■ Each party has different leadership/BOD and communication styles.<br>■ Empowerment is initiated. | ■ Each party may have informal knowledge portal (knowledge stores).<br>■ Each party has different vision/mission and communication styles.<br>■ Customer focus initiative may influence strategy. | ■ Each partner has its own performance management.<br>■ Partial service alliance agreement.<br>■ Part-time sharing of core business resource. | ■ EA process is informal.<br>■ Partial integration of application.<br>■ IT management processes are ad hoc and disorganized. |
| 2 | ■ Vague outline of the extended enterprise is emerging.<br>■ Commitment to future innovation and improvement is initiated.<br>■ Work team coordination starts. | ■ Some knowledge portals are shared by partners.<br>■ A consensus mission is built for an extended enterprise.<br>■ Customer satisfaction is focused in setting strategies. | ■ Customer perspective is shared.<br>■ Some goals are shared.<br>■ Partner's core business resource is shared. | ■ EA is under development.<br>■ Core application systems are integrated into management.<br>■ Processes follow a regular pattern. |
| 3 | ■ The scope of the extended enterprise is defined.<br>■ Shared values/direction/ performance expectation are defined.<br>■ High-performance work and environment are defined. | ■ Core knowledge portal for the extended enterprise is defined.<br>■ Vision/mission is defined for the extended enterprise.<br>■ Customer service level is defined. | ■ Balanced scorecard for performance management is defined.<br>■ CSF, KPI, and goals are defined.<br>■ Core business resource status is transparency/share. | ■ EA is defined.<br>■ Application management is fully implemented.<br>■ IT management processes are documented and communicated. |

**Exhibit 5.6  Maturity Model for the Extended Enterprise** (*Continued*)

| Level | Leadership | Vision | Change | Architecture |
|---|---|---|---|---|
| 4 | ▪ The scope change process is managed and measured.<br>▪ Catalyzes commitment and stimulates the group to high performance standards and innovation.<br>▪ Organizational learning process by CBT or IBT is implemented, and face-to-face case training is also provided. | ▪ Core knowledge portal is managed and measured.<br>▪ Strategy sharing occurs among partners.<br>▪ Customer complaints/claims are shared and monitored for customer expectation. | ▪ Performance management system is managed and measured.<br>▪ Ongoing monitoring goals are defined.<br>▪ Support process resource status transparency/share. | ▪ EA process is managed and measured.<br>▪ Application management is monitored.<br>▪ IT management processes are monitored and measured. |
| 5 | ▪ Continuous improvement of scope management occurs through knowledge portal.<br>▪ Paradoxical combination of personal humility and professional will become evident.<br>▪ Continuous learning program is fully implemented among partners and coaching and role model care systems also implemented for empowerment. | ▪ Knowledge portal is continuously improved for dynamic strategy process.<br>▪ Value/expectation are shared by all stakeholders involved throughout knowledge portal.<br>▪ Strategy formation goal is to exceed customer expectation. | ▪ Continuous strategy process for performance management.<br>▪ Ongoing strategy goals are defined.<br>▪ Knowledge portal clarifies status of all resources, including knowledge sharing. | ▪ Continuous improvement of EA through knowledge portal.<br>▪ Knowledge application management<br>▪ IT management best practices are followed and automated. |

all activities to identify the scope for improvements. This is designed to promote analysis and the identification of overlapping investments, gaps, and potential opportunities for collaboration within and across extended enterprises.

This enterprise index model is intended for use in analyzing investment in IT and other assets. It could also assist in future development of a broader architecture for a performance reporting/management system. The approach could define and communicate, for all interested stakeholders, a high-level view of how—in business terms—the extended enterprise can achieve its mission. Also, users of the index can identify how and where processes are being supported, where there are opportunities to reduce redundancies, and how to build more cost-effective solutions in the future.

## Performance Reference Model

Enterprises look to utilize a framework or criteria to tell them if they are on track with their expectations. A model for performance reference is just that, a framework that provides extended enterprises with a common measure across the entire enterprise. It allows all the partners involved in the extended enterprise to obtain a common view and shared reference point to evaluate the success or progress toward the overall targets or goals. A performance reference model will assist enterprises to more effectively and efficiently accomplish the following:

- Establish a common set of general performance outputs or measures that partners can use to help them achieve business goals and objectives.
- Articulate linkages between various internal and external components and the achievement of business and customer outcomes.
- Align various applications and enterprise architectures.
- Facilitate decisions on resource allocation issues.

By defining outcome measures, both the lines of business and the various partners involved with an extended enterprise can more readily be able to measure performance outcomes, and thus ensure future success. For a more detailed discussion of the various approaches that can be used to make up a performance reference model, see Appendix B.

## Matrix Evaluation Tools

To enable the leaders of an extended enterprise to govern effectively, it is necessary to set up a matrix setting out which parties of that enterprise, either the controlling one (owner) or an alliance partner, will carry out individual activities or functions within the wider extended enterprise. Using such a matrix helps identify and visually depicts responsibility. An example of such a matrix, in its most simple form, is illustrated in Exhibit 5.7. For this tool to provide the greatest value, the enterprise leaders need to be assured that the matrix is constantly up to date so they can easily mobilize people toward achieving the enterprise's vision, whatever the dynamic and changing environment may be at any point in time. Inevitably, partners and alliance members will also change with the enterprise's own evolution. A matrix of this index could involve the use of condition indicators (i.e., dashboard) that are used to highlight process responsibility and to call attention to the status of the enterprise's component activities if needed. The use of such a tool allows for easy and consistent evaluation of the condition indicators. This approach can be used to evaluate the condition of the enterprise's component activities, so as to direct the attention of leaders to those that require their intervention.

Another tool for evaluating the maturity of an enterprise's level of governance from a strategic perspective is illustrated in Exhibit 5.8. This enables members of the extended enterprise to know where core

**Exhibit 5.7　Matrix for the Scope of an Extended Enterprise**

| Partner / Function | A (OWN) | B | C | D | E | F |
|---|---|---|---|---|---|---|
| Marketing | ◯ | | | | ◯ | |
| Sales | ◯ | | | | | |
| Logistics | | | | ◯ | | |
| Manufacturing | | ◯ | | | | |
| Procurement | | | ◯ | | | |
| Resource support | | | | | | ◯ |

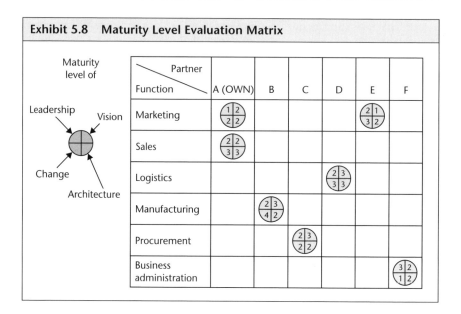

Exhibit 5.8   Maturity Level Evaluation Matrix

competencies, weakness, and risks exist, and allows them to be in a position to take action in a timely and informed manner. Knowing the maturity level of each activity's governance capabilities and of the associated condition monitoring systems allows all partners of the extended enterprise to make critical strategic decisions with confidence, despite the inherently flexible and transitory nature of the extended enterprise.

## SUMMARY

Among the key drivers, leadership has been identified as one of the most critical. For it is leadership that acts and empowers the knowledge as well as the processes. Other objectives to be considered are vision, change, and architecture. All of the objectives overlay or support the processes of an extended enterprise, namely business, support, and core processes. This chapter has focused squarely on the issues of governance challenges and approaches to structure, including the governance criteria needed to effectively participate in the business environment. It is vital that the enterprise must be concerned with governance for the organization, governance of intra-business entities, as well as interbusiness entities. There were various maturity models presented for the criteria, as well as a comparison of various global excellence models in existence.

# NOTES

1. *Enhancing Corporate Governance in Banking Organizations* (Basel, Switzerland: Bank for International Settlements, 1999).
2. *IT Control Objectives for Sarbanes-Oxley* (Rolling Meadows, IL: IT Governance Institute, 2004).
3. A. Bruce Pasternack and Albert J. Viscio, *The Centerless Corporation* (New York: Fireside, 1998).
4. The Malcolm Baldrige National Quality Award Program, National Institute of Standards and Technology (NIST), 2002.
5. Daniel Goleman, "Leadership that Gets Results," *Harvard Business Review* (March–April 2000).
6. Jim Collins, "Level 5 Leaderships: The Triumph of Humility and Fierce Resolve," *Harvard Business Review* (January 2001).

# 6

# ENTERPRISE ARCHITECTURE: GOVERNANCE IMPLEMENTATION FOR THE EXTENDED ENTERPRISE

## WHAT IS ENTERPRISE ARCHITECTURE?

Enterprise architecture is perhaps one of the hottest topics on the agenda of IT organizations. Hard decisions regarding resources, investments, information, applications, and technology all require enterprise architecture. Senior management views enterprise architecture as a critical component for making decisions that are consistent with the strategic plan for their organization. Just what is architecture and enterprise architecture? Architecture can be defined as a representation of a conceptual framework of components and their relationships at a point in time. Architecture discussions have been traditionally focused on technology issues. Enterprise architecture takes a broader view of business, matching it with the associated information.

## ENTERPRISE ARCHITECTURE: NEW FOCUS FOR CHIEF INFORMATION OFFICERS

Enterprise architecture provides the framework for ensuring that enterprisewide goals, objectives, and policies are properly and accurately reflected in decision making related to building, implementing, or changing information systems and to provide reasonable assurance that standards for interprocess communication, data naming, data representation, data structures, and information systems will be consistently and appropriately applied across the enterprise, including the extended enterprise. This has greatly changed the focus of the chief information officers (CIOs). This focus on enterprise architecture now requires CIOs to assume the governance responsibility of ensuring that enterprise architecture is used to identify problems addressed by architecture and uses the architecture to do the following:

- *Make decisions.* CIOs must assume governance responsibility to ensure that information systems are in place and information is available to enhance the enterprise's ability to guide decision making and interprocess communication, as well as ensuring that information systems will be consistently or appropriately applied across the enterprise.

- *Manage change.* Since the introduction of IT quickens the pace of change within enterprises, CIOs and IT managers must ensure that IT is able to deal with the high rate of change in today's complex information environment, understands the effect of any given change in the enterprise, and manages the change to accurately represent the enterprise's goals, objectives, and policies, as well as ensuring that the functionality of information systems can continue to provide accurate information across the enterprise at the same level of service availability and at different points in time.

- *Improve communications.* As part of the enterprise architecture, the CIO or IT manager will ensure that information systems have a clear picture of the interrelationship among the systems and adequately communicate the linkages between the systems. The consequences could be a missed opportunity of sharing data, different definition and naming used for the same data, or the same name for different data.

- *Ensure information technology is acquired and information resources are managed to be consistent with business planning.* The enterprise has objectives and a strategic plan to meet these objectives. If the enterprise architecture supports the business strategies and enables rapid change, benefits will accrue. When the architecture constrains business activities, the enterprise could risk creating a short-term solution with long-term support cost or not be capable of providing senior management with the information needed to manage the enterprise. Further, the CTO, CIO, or IT manager must be able to keep current with the capability of new technologies, and advise senior management on how new technology could facilitate business change. When the CEO asks an IT question, the CIO or CTO will need to be able to answer it correctly, and in business terms that the CEO or senior management will understand.

An example of the new focus of the CIO and IT manager is the enactment of the Clinger-Cohen Act,[1] which has been implemented by the Chief Information Officer (CIO) Council of the U.S. federal government. The Act was developed to provide a comprehensive approach for managing future IT investments. To ensure all departments and agencies of the government are following the council's directions, all are instructed to begin using the generally accepted (IT focused) enterprise architecture.

The CIO Council's enterprise architecture (EA)[2] provides an explicit description of the existing and desired relationships between business and information technology. It is designed to assist in setting direction on such issues as the promotion of interoperability, open systems, public access, end-user satisfaction, and security. The EA describes the relationships between the work, various business units, and the information required and supported by IT infrastructure. It follows the five-component enterprise architecture framework model and is now being used when developing, maintaining and implementing new systems. This example may assist those entities looking to improve their governance systems and infrastructure in the extended enterprise environment.

Much greater emphasis is placed on business and information requirements. This in turn effectively supports the business and enables information sharing across different business units or so-called traditional barriers. The organization's ability to deliver effective and timely services is also enhanced and supports the organization's effort to improve its underlying functions and services. As stated by W. Bradford Rigdon, "a discussion of architecture" from the enterprise architecture perspective, "must take into account different *layers* of architecture. These layers can be illustrated by a pyramid, with the business unit at the top and the delivery system at the base," as shown in Exhibit 6.1. An enterprise is composed of one or more business units that are responsible for a specific business area.[3] In the United States, the National Association of State CIOs (NASCIO) Enterprise Architecture Development Tool–Kit[4] further states, "Adopting enterprise architecture increases the utility of an enterprise's data by facilitating information sharing between data stores. Committing to an ongoing renewable enterprise architecture process fosters a technology-adaptive enterprise. Enterprise architecture becomes a road map, guiding all future technology investments and

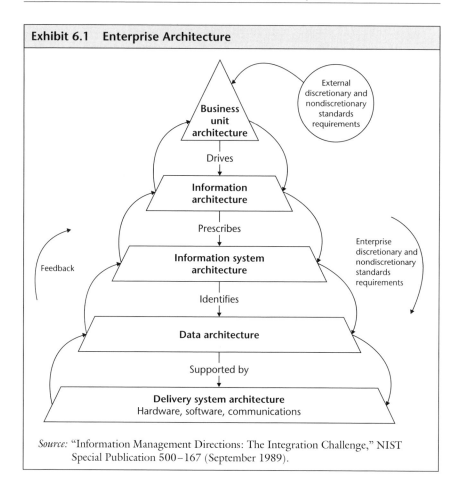

**Exhibit 6.1    Enterprise Architecture**

*Source:* "Information Management Directions: The Integration Challenge," NIST
Special Publication 500–167 (September 1989).

identifying and aiding in the resolution of gaps in the entity's business
and IT infrastructures."[5]

Typical enterprise architecture is the inclusive term used to describe
the following five layers of architecture:

1. *Business unit architecture:* Business processes
2. *Information architecture:* Information flows and relationships
3. *Information systems architecture:* Applications
4. *Data architecture:* Data descriptions
5. *Delivery system architecture:* Technology infrastructure

These five levels of enterprise architecture were first introduced in 1989
by the U.S. National Institute of Standards (NIST). They remain valid and
can be readily applied in today's extended enterprise environment. The

U.S. Federal Enterprise Architecture Framework was developed by the U.S. Chief Information Officers (CIO) Council, who agreed to use this NIST model and expand on this foundation to meet the organizational and management needs.[6] The five-layered model was able to allow for organizing, planning, and building an integrated set of information and information technology architecture. The following is a common description for each of the layers.

## Business Unit Architecture

The business unit architecture (business processes) component describes the core business processes that support the organization's missions. Components for the business unit architecture generally focus on external and internal reporting requirements and functional areas. From the discretionary standards perspective that an enterprise may select as part of its architecture, standards could be based on policies used by like industries, both nationally and internationally: standards that would provide reusability of assets and migration from the current environment to a proposed environment, as well as standards for information sharing. From the mandatory standards perspective, an enterprise must adhere to best business practices and legislations.

The component of this architecture is a high-level analysis of the work performed in support of the enterprise's mission, vision, and goals. Business processes can be described by decomposing the processes into derivative business activities. Analysis of the business processes determines the information needed and processed by the organization. Each business process should incorporate performance management structure by itself—namely, plan, do, check, and act cycle, as presented in Chapter 3.

## Information Architecture

The information architecture (information flows and relationships) component analyzes the information used by the organization in its business processes, identifying the information used and the movement of the information within the organization. Components of this architecture include original documents, data, revisions, and responsible organizations. The discretionary standards include security standards, rules, and procedures to ensure information integrity, naming conventions, and description methods. The nondiscretionary standards to which an enterprise must adhere are the government and/or industry regulatory requirements.

Relationships among the various flows of information are also described in this component and indicate where the information is needed and how the information is shared to support mission functions. This level represents technical and management information flow, as well as the impact of time on information integrity and meaning.

## Information Systems Architecture

The information systems architecture (application) identifies, defines, and organizes the activities that capture, manipulate, and manage the business information to support mission operations, as well as the logical dependencies and relationships among business activities. It establishes a framework to meet the specific information requirements given by the information architecture. It uses its components to acquire and process data, shows the automated and procedure-oriented information system that supports the information flow, and produces and distributes information according to the architecture requirements and standards.

Components for information systems architecture refer to specifications, requirements, applications, modules, databases, and procedures. Discretionary or nonmandatory components could be information systems development approaches such as an object-oriented approach, inquiry and application development languages such as the use of JAVA or ActiveX methodologies for designing the processing and data flow and the architecture for the system from the network standards, or hardware and software standards to the database standards. Nondiscretionary or mandatory components would be the enterprise's software development standards.

## Data Architecture

The data architecture (data description and relationships) identifies how data are maintained, accessed, and utilized. At a high level, it defines the data and describes the relationship among data elements in the organization's information systems. It also interfaces to the application system component to store or locate information required for processing or for subsequent storage by application systems. Components for this architecture layer can include data models that describe the nature of the data underlying the business and information needs, such as physical database design, database and file structures, data definitions, data dictionaries, and data elements that underlie the information systems of the enterprise. It is important to minimize redundancy and to support new applications. Discretionary standards that the enterprise may select as part of the architecture are naming conventions and file and database compatibility, especially in the areas of interprocess sharing. Since the data architecture concentrates on data description and relationships within the system, there are no known nondiscretionary or mandatory standards for this architecture layer.

## Delivery System Architecture

The delivery system architecture (technology and communication infrastructure) describes and identifies the information service layer, network service layer, and components, including the functional characteristics, capabilities, and interconnections of the hardware, software, and communications (networks, protocols, and nodes). It represents the wiring diagram of the physical IT infrastructure and facility support requirements so that they could properly accommodate and connect these assets in an integrated manner. Discretionary standards for this layer that an enterprise may select are the OSI standards, data interchange standards, hardware, network and portal architectures, and optical storage. Similar to the data architecture layer, because the components are related to technology and communication infrastructure, there are no known nondiscretionary or mandatory standards for this layer. However, as governments have begun to address legislation concerning doing business on the Internet (such as enactment of a consumption tax for online purchasing), nondiscretionary or mandatory standards for delivery systems architecture could be adopted for consistency in delivery of information to regulatory bodies.

## ARCHITECTURE LAYERS INTERRELATIONSHIPS

These architecture layers are mutually interdependent and interrelated. For example, the first four layers are logically connected and related in a top-down dependency. The delivery system is the foundation of the architecture and is dependent on the definition of the business goals and objectives. An architecture may be a description of one of these layers at a particular point of time, and may represent a view of a current situation with islands of automation, redundant processes, and data inconsistencies. It can also be a representation of future integrated automation information structure or end state that is in the enterprise's migration plan and gives context and guidance for future activities.

Enterprise architecture layers are vital for effective establishment of e-commerce systems (application systems), databases (information repositories/stores), and for e-portals (communications infrastructure) in support of the extended enterprise. There can be much complexity and numerous components in enterprise, and the interrelationship between the components and the implementation steps must be understood in order to formulate a consistent business plan and to govern effectively. In other words, an enterprise architecture can be described as the knowledge that drives the business, the information necessary to operate the business, the technologies necessary to support the business operations, and the overall processes necessary for implementing IT to respond to the changing needs of business. The development and implementation of enterprise architecture is a vital first step for all enterprises, whether commercial or governmental, that plan to conduct business in the twenty-first century. Establishing enterprise architecture, as stated previously, can provide a high-level view of the business and information requirements and enhances the enterprise's ability to guide decision making and manage change. It can also be used to communicate the organization's goals, objectives, and policies throughout the organization.

## IMPLEMENTING AND MAINTAINING THE ENTERPRISE ARCHITECTURE

After establishing a framework for the enterprise architecture, one of the critical areas that need to be focused on is prioritizing areas of high incremental benefits for early implementation. The following areas should be considered:

- *Change management.* Enterprise architecture must continuously evolve in support of changes in business functions. Thus, enterprise architecture itself should be managed with the same change control process that governs other critical documents, including databases/graphical depictions.

- *Legacy systems integration.* Enterprise architecture needs to realistically account for the existing infrastructure base, including legacy systems as well as systems that are currently in use. The architectural representation should pay greater focus on interoperability with the interfaces between legacy systems and new systems. If the interface to the legacy systems does not conform to the architecture, the organization will need to decide whether to change, replace, or terminate the process based on cost or operational or functional effectiveness criteria.

- *IT personnel planning.* Enterprise architecture should reflect the training procedures and staffing needed to support its successful implementation. It is critical to include plans for the remediation of deficiencies, including strategies and plans for skill acquisition, new capability development, hiring and training, and for ongoing professional development of existing employees.

- *Enterprise architecture compliance, waivers, and certification.* Configuration management and control as well as quality software engineering processes for systems integration should be implemented to maintain consistency with sound architectural design. Configuration changes should be tested and validated prior to acceptance for use across the architecture.

## INFORMATION TECHNOLOGY GOVERNANCE IN THE EXTENDED ENTERPRISE

Governance development has been driven primarily by the need for transparency of enterprise risks and the protection of shareholder value. The pervasive use of information, systems, and technology has created a critical dependency on IT and requires specific focus on IT governance. IT governance plays an important part in the total governance responsibility of the board of directors and executive management and is an integral part of enterprise governance. Leadership and their associated organizational structures are needed to ensure that the organization's IT can sustain and extend the organization's strategies and objectives. As stated in the CobiT *Management Guidelines,*[7] IT governance is a system of control that ensures the business objectives are achieved. This usually consists of directing the organization's IT endeavors after reviewing its reported performance against some norms, which call for the following:

- Strategic IT infrastructure to enable the business and maximize its benefits
- Maturity model of the enterprise architecture/IT architecture to ensure IT resources are being used responsibly
- Partner ability for networking/information flows and relationships
- Maturity model for IT governance
- Information and data model for quick knowledge base implementation

## STRATEGIC ALIGNMENT OF IT STRATEGIES WITH THE BUSINESS

Why is an enterprise business strategy so important to an IT strategy? IT, which has long been considered solely as the enabler of an enterprise, is now regarded as an integral part of business strategy. In a recent Gartner research paper, "Six Building Blocks for Creating Real IT Strategies," authors Robert Mack and Ned Frey stated, "A focused driven business strategy will lead to the most efficient application of IT expenses. In the best case, each project selected for implementation will, to a significant degree, be justified by its contribution to the overall strategy, becoming a link in a chain of projects over time that are directed toward achieving a strategic objective."[8]

This is especially true in the extended environment where knowledge sharing is the key concern of the competency. Strategic alignment between IT and enterprise objectives is a critical success factor. It is an integral part of the knowledge management and business strategy itself. The overall governance structure should include coverage of the extent of strategic alignment of IT with business activities among the partners of the extended enterprise. This relationship is illustrated in Exhibit 6.2.

IT should *support* the enterprise strategies and should not be in a position of *making* its enterprise strategies. A business strategy is necessary for any effective IT strategy. This involves seeking out factors for

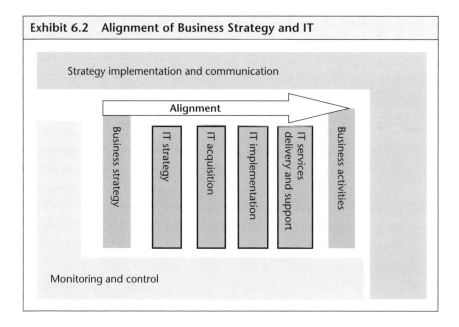

**Exhibit 6.2    Alignment of Business Strategy and IT**

Strategy implementation and communication

Alignment

Business strategy

IT strategy

IT acquisition

IT implementation

IT services delivery and support

Business activities

Monitoring and control

defining decisions. For example, IT strategy must align with the business strategy. Further, any IT strategic plan such as acquisition, implementation, and IT services, delivery, and support must be aligned and support the respective business plan. In turn, these strategies and IT activities must be aligned in support of business activities. Business strategies must be properly and timely communicated between all the resources involved. Monitoring and controls must also be in place to ensure that strategies are coevolving and patching to meet the business activities. Performance measurements should be implemented to ensure that the business strategies and objectives are accomplished.

## IT INFRASTRUCTURE TO ENABLE BUSINESS

The purpose of IT governance is to direct IT endeavors to ensure that performance meets the following objectives:

- IT activities are aligned with the business
- Value delivery of IT
- IT resources management
- Business and IT-related risks are being managed appropriately
- Performance measurement of IT

For example, the CIOs of all departments and agencies of the U.S. federal government are required to implement a technical model for enterprise architecture to ensure that all departments and agencies of the government are following this technical reform model (TRM), allowing for better control and coordinated development, acquisition, interoperability, and support of all its IT systems.

The governance approach relies on the development, collection, and utilization of *enterprise elements* consisting of information developed and documented by both the business and IT communities within the enterprise. Information contained in these enterprise elements becomes the foundation for building the enterprise architecture. Enterprise elements can be strategic or procedural, as well as tactical.

Strategic elements provide top-down communication within the enterprise to ensure that enterprise-level strategies are being addressed. Strategic elements include the enterprise direction, mission statements, organizational charts, operational budgets, strategies, goals, objectives, and strategic initiatives.

Procedural elements provide the translation of communications from top down as well as bottom up, identifying the implementation relationships. Some of the procedural elements are project methodologies, service policies and procedures, and adaptive enterprise architecture.

Tactical elements provide information from the bottom up and the actual delivery of the various services, products, and initiatives. Management can measure the effectiveness of the architecture efforts. Some of the tactical elements are tactical initiatives, services, projects, and budgets.

Architecture governance roles can be defined in two categories—primary and supportive. The primary roles include overseer, champion, manager, documenter, communicator, reviewer, advisor, and listener. The supportive role can be subject matter experts, project team members, special interest groups, and enterprise executives.

Governance should provide the basic architecture structure for IT elements. Whether the infrastructure serves the entire enterprise or is limited to a particular business unit, service and applications deliverables should be integrated or decentralized products. Sourcing for the IT application and operation strategies should ensure that they are built to meet the enterprise's short- and long-term business strategies. Business units are accountable for their business processes, and all changes that support these processes must be reviewed and approved by a central group to ensure a clear line of accountability, as well as close cooperation between the business operations function and the support function.

Governance should also focus on processes from end to end. As functions within a workplace extend to third parties or outsourcing of the business processes, organizations must manage the entire process results and not just those provided within the organization.

## MATURITY MODEL OF THE ENTERPRISE ARCHITECTURE/IT ARCHITECTURE

Following the guidance of the U.S. CIO Council, the U.S. Department of Commerce developed an enterprisewide IT architecture (i.e., enterprise architecture plus a technical reference model and standard profiles). This step was taken in order to possess a highly adaptive and enabling infrastructure that reduces integration complexity and lowers the total cost of ownership. The Commerce Department wanted to ensure continued progress building on previous efforts and to fully realize the benefits of its IT architecture.

To effectively structure management actions arising from analysis of the current architecture, the Commerce Department developed an IT enterprise architecture maturity model, as shown in Exhibit 6.3. The objective of this model is to enhance the overall odds for success of the IT architecture by identifying weak areas. It can be looked at as a good first step within an extended enterprise to provide a defined path toward improvement. As an architecture approach matures, it should increase

| **Exhibit 6.3   Maturity Model for the Enterprise Architecture** | | |
| --- | --- | --- |
| *Level* | *Focus* | *Characteristics* |
| 0 | No enterprise architecture program. | No enterprise architecture |
| 1 | **Initial**—Informal enterprise architecture process is under way. | Processes are ad hoc and informal. Some enterprise architecture processes are defined. There is no unified architecture process across technologies and lines of business. Success depends on individual efforts. Quality of work is inconsistent. There is little communication about the enterprise architecture process and possible improvements. |
| 2 | Enterprise architecture process is **Under Development.** | Basic enterprise architecture process program is documented based on Office of Management and Budget Circular A-130 and U.S. Department of Commerce enterprise architecture guidance. Responsibilities are assigned and work is underway. The architecture process has developed clear roles and responsibilities. There is a clear understanding of where the organization is at the present time. Business and IT vision, combined principles, baselines, and targets are identified. |
| 3 | **Defined**—Enterprise architecture includes detailed diagrams and technical reference model to promote common understanding. | The architecture is defined and communicated. The process is largely followed. Gap analysis, migration plan, technical reference model, standards profile, and migration plan are completed. Cost-benefits are considered in identifying projects. IT goals and methods are identified. Training and awareness programs are provided at regular intervals. Enterprise architecture is integrated with strategic planning and budgeting processes. |
| | | *(continues)* |

| Exhibit 6.3 *(Continued)* | | |
|---|---|---|
| *Level* | *Focus* | *Characteristics* |
| 4 | Enterprise architecture process is **Managed** and measured. | Enterprise architecture is used to guide development and acquisition. Enterprise architecture is updated on a regular cycle to refresh the architecture content and to adjust the strategic planning and budgeting processes based on the feedback received and lessons learned. Enterprise architecture projects are reviewed against architecture standards. Opportunities associated with the architecture process are captured. Organizational personnel understand the architecture and its uses. |
| 5 | The continuous improvement of enterprise architecture process is **Optimized.** | Opportunity analysis is used to drive continuous process improvements in enterprise architecture. The process feeds business process reengineering and other characteristics. |

*Source:* U.S. Department of Commerce.

the benefits it offers the organization. The model delineates an evolutionary way to improve the overall process from commencement through to maturity, looking at any gaps.

Additional detail related to a maturity model for enterprise architecture/IT architecture management can be found in Appendix G, "Enterprise Architecture Processes at Different Maturity Levels."

## PARTNER ABILITY FOR NETWORKING/INFORMATION FLOWS AND RELATIONSHIPS

The success of an extended enterprise will be measured by the extent to which it delivers its agreed strategies matching its vision and mission. Furthermore, this ability will need to be continuously upgraded as it faces the twin competitive pressures: to raise the quality of products/ services required and, at the same time, to reduce costs. Consider the air travel industry. In the initial phase, airlines basically shared a reservation system and allowed passengers to share in other frequent-flyer programs. This progressed rapidly to code sharing and comarketing of joint frequent-flyer programs, such as the STAR Alliance program jointly shared among Air New Zealand, All Nippon Airways, Austrian Airlines, Lufthansa, Air Canada, SAS, Singapore Airlines, Thai Airways International, Varig and United Airlines, etc., and ONE WORLD alliance program jointly shared among American Airlines, British Airways, Aer Lingus, Cathay Pacific, Finnair, Iberia, Qantas, and a few smaller airlines. The sharing of flight schedules was the next level achieved in the alliance programs. The next stage in the networking will be an even closer integration of products/services to augment the collaborative arrangements and sustain customer loyalty, perhaps, to the extent of operating multiple partners under a single alliance brand. Another opportunity will be to share infrastructure costs, utilize partner's processes and networks if superior to their own, and make optimal use of fixed assets (presumably aircraft and hangars).

Effective exchange and collection of useful information (knowledge/ context) among the partners/stockholders in an extended enterprise is critical. However, many times the capability and capacity of the business processes, governance, and IT of the various partners of an extended enterprise varies significantly. As such, there is a direct relationship between information sharing and governance capabilities and the capacity of the partners to work effectively in an extended enterprise. Using the maturity level concepts that were presented in COBIT,[9] Exhibit 6.4 presents the underpinnings of just what is required for effective business partner collaboration. An initial step to forming an effective extended enterprise is to assess the governance maturity level of each proposed partner in the network. The maturity level of the business partners may limit the extent to which networking evolves.

The detail maturity model of information sharing and governance for each business process is addressed in Appendix H.

## MATURITY MODEL FOR IT GOVERNANCE

The *Maturity Model for IT Governance,* published by the IT Governance Institute as a part of COBIT, provides a defined set of maturity levels for information and related technology controls addressing these profiles. Sections of the model can be found in Appendix J of this publication. The IT Governance Institute has also provided technical guidance for the Net-centric environment in *Control Objectives for Net Centric Technology.*[10] This guideline provides well-structured ways of understanding and assessing the network environment and a quick guide for management and IT professionals when addressing controls within this environment.

| Exhibit 6.4 | Maturity Level Table for Extended Enterprise Partner Candidates | |
|---|---|---|
| *Level* | *Focus* | *Characteristics* |
| **0** Not ready | Impossible | It is impossible to get into effective partnerships, as there is a complete lack of information systems through which useful information about customers and products/services relationships can be generated or exchanged. |
| **1** Partial integration | Ad hoc | High risk. There is a possibility of networking only if the partners agree to outsource entire information systems and business processes of the core business to one of the most competent partners in the extended enterprise. |
| **2** Core systems integrated management | Intuitive | With strong leadership, management may contract for limited partnerships within an extended enterprise, but it may require significant empowerment of employees. |
| **3** Fully integrated management | Defined/integrated | Contracts clarify overall accountability and key performance indicators among partners, and partners are rewarded based on performance against key performance indicators across the enterprise. |
| **4** Monitoring management | Controlled/measurable | Contracts extend to the core resource sharing level, and monitoring systems have started to be implemented by the partners. There is a clear focus on the identity of world-class levels for products/services. |
| **5** Knowledge management | Ideal/optimized | Contracts extend to the knowledge-sharing level to meet the customers' expectations on a continuous basis. |

## ESTABLISH INFORMATION MODEL AND DATA MODEL FOR QUICK IMPLEMENTATION OF A KNOWLEDGE BASE

Business leaders today have the highest expectations that products providing solutions will be implemented in a matter of days, not months, to meet the globally highly competitive environment. Additionally, all business partners of an extended enterprise have the expectation of sufficient high-level IT capabilities among the other members of the partnership.

How effectively and quickly entities can implement these knowledge bases and information systems has become a critical issue for an extended enterprise. The extended enterprise should have a clear picture of the information and data model (contents and relationships of the useful information) for the partners within the extended enterprises, as indicated by the relevant layers within the enterprise architecture. Each partner may efficiently and effectively collaborate for implementing or cosharing database or systems design with this information model.

Governance over an extended enterprise can be extremely complex. This publication has attempted to capture and summarize some of the experience, which points to the overriding need for an EA approach (showing the issues in clear charts and diagrams) as the best route to achieving successful and effective governance.

## SUMMARY

An EA approach now requires CIOs, CTOs, or IT managers to assume the governance responsibility of ensuring that enterprise architecture is used to identify problems addressed by architecture and uses the architecture to advise and assist senior management in not only making decisions but also to assist in managing change. Since concepts were presented for an architecture approach, issues of a maturity model for dealing with enterprise architecture, as well as a sample maturity model for IT governance, the enterprise that is determined to participate in the extended environment should begin to feel more prepared. Utilizing a consistent architectural approach will offer highly effective guidance when working to align the IT infrastructure with the governance of information technology. Gartner and others are predicting that enterprise architecture will continue to grow in importance. Certainly by 2007 it will rank as one of the most important issues with which the CIO and CTO will need to be concerned with as they approach their responsibilities.

## NOTES

1. U.S. Information Technology Management Reform Act, "Clinger-Cohen Act," enacted January 1996.
2. Federal Enterprise Architecture System, Chief Information Council, Washington, DC, 1999.
3. W. Bradford Rigdon, "Information Management Directions: The Integration Challenge," Chapter 7 in *Architecture and Standards* (Gaithersburg,

MD: NIST, Information Systems Engineering Division, U.S. Department of Commerce, National Technical Information Service, 1989).

4. "Enterprise Architecture Development Tool-Kit," V2.0, *Adaptive Enterprise Architecture Development Program,* National Association of State CIOs, July 2002.

5. *Ibid.*

6. Federal Enterprise Architecture Framework, Version 1.1, The Chief Information Security Council, September 1999.

7. COBIT *Management Guidelines* (Rolling Meadows, IL: IT Governance Institute, July 2000).

8. Robert Mack and Ned Frey, "Six Building Blocks for Creating Real IT Strategies," Gartner Group, 2002.

9. COBIT (Rolling Meadows, IL: IT Governance Institute, July 2000).

10. *Control Objectives Net Centric Technology, Intranet/Extranet/Internet* (Rolling Meadows, IL: IT Governance Institute, 1999).

# APPENDIX A

# QUESTIONS FOR THE BOARD AND SENIOR MANAGEMENT

The purpose of this appendix is to provide a list of suggested questions that organizations may want to ask themselves when looking to assess the effectiveness and readiness to participate in an extended environment. As previously discussed, in today's extended enterprise environment, organizations have stretched their operations to the outside. This leverages the connectivity of the Internet through portals and common languages and offers uninterrupted services using Web technology. The traditional big iron organization structures have moved to a distributed environment where the four walls become no walls, and the inward processing structure has expanded to include business partners, suppliers, and perhaps customers. Under the enterprise architecture, data can be input into the system touchpoints anywhere on the Internet. The goal of the enterprise architecture is to replace the corporate walls with portals, gateways, and conduits that bring it all together.

The key to successful enterprise architecture implementation is to make technology serve the business better, while keeping pace with business change. This may require a constructive tearing down of the walls within the IT infrastructure that impede the flow of information, while building capabilities that increase it, as well as a change in information management directions and focuses. As stated in the Introduction of this book, enterprise architecture represents a major new knowledge resource, as well as opening new avenues of practice in strategy setting, enterprise management control assessment, and risk management. It also provides assurance that the IT strategies are aligned with the business strategies and business activities. Further, the IT strategies are being reviewed periodically to ensure that they are aligned with the business strategies, that the business strategies are aligned with business activities, and that ongoing communications, monitoring, and control exist throughout the organization.

## GOVERNANCE AND MANAGEMENT OF ENTERPRISE ARCHITECTURES

Creating processes for the management and governance of the extended enterprise is as important as building architecture. Issues of governance form some of the most important aspects if success is to be achieved in the implementation of enterprise architecture for the extended enterprise. As discussed in the text, there are five areas in the extended enterprise that require governance and management attention. The five areas that should be addressed during the planning and implementation phase of the organization, transition phase as well as postimplementation, are as follows:

1. Strategy
2. IT governance
3. Performance management
4. Operational business activities
5. Enterprise architecture

## GOVERNANCE AND MANAGEMENT QUESTIONS

The business model defines the governance responsibilities. The measure of whether the governance structure is adequate would require examining whether the decision makers in the chain of governance have the appropriate span of control. For example, if the strategy requires cooperation of all the business units and partners involved but there is no decision maker in place to make that happen, the potential for success of implementing the IT strategies would probably be low.

One of the most frequently asked questions by senior management and the boards is this: How can I tell if the governance and management structure is adequate to ensure IT strategies are aligned with the business strategies in the extended enterprise? What follows is a list of questions that may be used as a guide to ensure that key components for the extended enterprise have been addressed.

## STRATEGY

A strategy enables the organization to become more effective in recommending and deploying appropriate technologies in support of the IT infrastructure. The lack of strategy could leave the organization in a dilemma in managing enterprise IT expectation, and with no clear vision for directing their investments. Further, the deployment of IT infrastructure may not be agile to meet changes in business strategies, while effectively communicating with partners, suppliers, and customers.

To achieve great strategic outcomes, visionary leaders must encourage emerging and enabling value innovation. Does the strategy for the extended enterprise include:

- Continual focus on creating value through innovation?
- Continual strategy process—evolving, linking, and patching?
- Effective sharing of knowledge required to govern the enterprise through the use of a knowledge portal?
- Effective communication of managed knowledge throughout the organization that provides actionable outcome?
- Strategic framework focus on:
  - □ Analyzing information to understand the organization's position in terms of meeting the business goals?
  - □ Identifying competitive advantage?
  - □ Defining the products and markets?
  - □ Identifying the core business on which the organization should focus?
  - □ Identifying, prioritizing, and implementing change?
  - □ Continuously monitoring performance and reviewing strategy?
- Strategic planning process involving everyone on the team in gathering information?
- Balance between short- and long-term thinking?
- Internal governance strategy to match the changing requirements of the external and internal environments facing the enterprise?

## IT GOVERNANCE

Governance has the greatest impact on the outcome of strategies. Integration of decisions and business processes generally represent the key constraints a business model can place on any strategy, whether it involves information technology or not. In the extended enterprise environment, where information and function sharing has extended to all involved business units, governance must focus on IT elements such as the IT structure, service delivery approach, application, and sourcing strategies.

These questions should be asked:

- Is the IT governance a component of the overall governance model?
- Does the governance model include structure, objectives, goals and expectations, enterprise activities, and tangible and intangible resources?
- Do the governance objectives include:
  □ Leadership?
  □ Vision?
  □ Change?
  □ Architecture?
- Has the governance criteria been established for the extended enterprise?
- Do the governance criteria focus on values for the business process, support process, core process, and tangible as well as intangible resources?
- Has the stakeholder value been considered when setting overall strategy?
- Does the IT governance address:
  □ IT alignment with the business?
  □ IT infrastructure to enable the business and maximize its benefits?
  □ Maturity model existence to ensure IT resources are being used responsibly?
  □ Partner ability for networking, and information flows and relationships?
- Do IT governance initiatives match with the decision-making style of the enterprise?
- Are the IT governance mechanisms fully integrated and continuously evolved?
- Have performance measurements, such as the use of balanced scorecard, been implemented to measure the effectiveness of IT governance?

- Have procedures been implemented to inform enterprise members of the measurement results and that the results are acted upon?

- Has a maturity model been established and implemented for evaluating the level of governance of the extended enterprise?

## PERFORMANCE MANAGEMENT AND MEASUREMENT

Architecture for the performance measurement process as presented by the IT Governance Institute (ITGI)[1] contains various functions: objective setting, providing directions for the IT activities, measuring performance, and comparing the results from the IT activity to the objectives. The results from the comparison may require redirection of activities where necessary and change of objectives where appropriate. Set objectives should include alignment with business strategies, maximizing the benefits and proper management of the IT-related risks. IT activities, however, must increase automation to maximize benefits, decrease cost to enhance the enterprise efficiency (as well as manage risks associated with security and reliability of the process), and be in compliance with the corporate policies, standards, and legal requirements.

These questions should be asked:

- Has a performance management process been established to measure and compare the performance to the objectives, to provide redirection of business activities where necessary, and change of objectives as appropriate?

- Do performance measurements include:
  - Measures in terms of what customers and stakeholders want?
  - The process of delivering reliable, cost-effective, high-quality IT products and services?
  - Use of SWOT (strength, weakness, opportunities, and threat) approach to analyze the strength and weaknesses of the organization and an analysis between the internal and external (business partners)?
  - CSFs to identify the most critical processes/resources needed to accomplish business goals?
  - Ongoing strategy process and operational performance monitoring?

- Are the results generated by the process both timely and useful?

- Are the generated results discussed and acted upon for the betterment of the enterprise?

## OPERATIONAL BUSINESS ACTIVITIES

In the extended enterprise, management must capture innovation with business partners at the global and local levels and share the innovation throughout the extended enterprise. It should be used to further develop world-class products and services. The organizational environment must resemble a network of distributed intelligence and the enterprise's business strategies must include multiple perspectives, customs, and business environments. Major challenges in this environment include consensus building and managerial transformation. The scope of the blueprint for knowledge sharing includes all stakeholders (customers, partners, suppliers, etc.). A core knowledge portal should be available for all stakeholders within the extended enterprise. For each enterprise, a knowledge portal should be provided for compartmentalization of knowledge activities. Potential strategic partners and potential alliances with other knowledge portals are outside the scope.

Operational business activities are based on directions/orders/origination generated from information sharing. Such activities frequently involve the use of tangible resources such as core business activities relating to the flow of products and/or services. These may include purchasing, production, marketing, and distribution activities. Strategy setting and subordinate action plans governing operational activities are derived after the analysis of information/knowledge and decision making in information sharing activities. An organization's future success is dependent on its people's knowledge, skill, creativity, and motivation. Governance systems in the extended enterprise are focusing on the orderly distribution of power and authority in the service of developing more competitive and responsible enterprises. A sound governance structure should be implemented to provide an environment that meets these conditions and to realize the values.

The following questions should be asked:

- As enterprises begin to collaborate more extensively with partners and customers, significant changes in operations may be necessary as the operations architectures become more complex. Has the operations framework addressed:
  - □ The need to create knowledge sharing and establishing knowledge portals?

- ☐ Creation of knowledge management process, including goal relationships, core business relationships, resource relationships, and knowledge relationships?

- ☐ Information sharing activities, a two-way communication process between management and all stakeholders in building a common culture, acceptance, and ownership of its mission and strategy?

- Has a blueprint been used for knowledge sharing, including:

  - ☐ Missions translated into goals and objectives?

  - ☐ Actions of individuals aligned and supportive of the organization?

  - ☐ A continuum with the vision, mission, and values of the extended enterprise?

- Are the roles and responsibilities in the areas of problem resolutions and change management properly identified?

- Are collaborations within the enterprise architecture effective and intact?

## ENTERPRISE ARCHITECTURE

Enterprise architecture implementation increases the utility of an enterprise's data by facilitating information sharing between various data stores. Committing to an ongoing renewable enterprise architecture process fosters a technology-adaptive enterprise. Enterprise architecture thus becomes a road map for guiding future technology investments and in identifying and aiding the resolution of gaps in the entity's business and IT infrastructures.

The following questions should be asked:

- Does the enterprise architecture fully support the business organizational objectives?

- Is the CIO assuming the responsibility of ensuring that enterprise architecture is used to identify problems addressed by architecture and uses it to advise and assist senior management in:

  - ☐ Making decisions?

  - ☐ Managing change?

  - ☐ Improving communications?

  - ☐ Ensuring information technology?

- □ Acquiring information technology and managing information resources to be consistent with business planning?
- ■ Has the enterprise architecture addressed:
  - □ Business unit architecture (business process)?
  - □ Information architecture (information flows and relationships)?
  - □ Information systems architecture (applications)?
  - □ Data architecture (data descriptions)?
  - □ Delivery system architecture (technology infrastructure)?
- ■ Has the framework for enterprise architecture take into consideration prioritizing areas of high incremental benefits for early implementation?

## NOTE

1. *Board Briefing on IT Governance,* 2nd edition (Rolling Meadows, IL: IT Governance Institute, October 2003).

# APPENDIX B

# PERFORMANCE REFERENCE MODEL

This appendix describes some of the performance reference models covered in Chapter 5.

## SIX SIGMA PERFORMANCE MANAGEMENT TOOL

*Six Sigma* is a way of measuring processes and a new approach to business. This new approach impacts the habits that drive an organization. It was pioneered by Motorola, but has since been adopted by all types of organizations, be they manufacturing or service related. Six Sigma is a goal of near-perfection and an approach to changing the culture of an organization. In other words, it is a broad and comprehensive system for building and sustaining business performance success and leadership. Six Sigma is a context within which one will be able to integrate many valuable but often disconnected management *best practices* and concepts—including systems thinking, continuous improvement, knowledge management, mass customization, and activity-based management. The type of business success that one may achieve is broad because of the many proven benefits. Examples of the benefits of the Six Sigma system, as stated in the *Six-Sigma Way* by Per S. Pande, Robert P. Neuman, and Roland R. Cavanagh,[1] include:

- Cost reduction
- Productivity improvement
- Market-share growth

- Customer retention
- Cycle-time reduction
- Defect reduction
- Culture change
- Product/service development

From the personal experience of those on the research team, an organization that has participated in the Six Sigma approach should embrace the following themes:

- Customer focus puts customer's needs first, backed by systems and strategies that will tie the business to the voice of the customer.

- Data and fact-driven management use effective measurement systems to track both results and outcomes and other predictive factors.

- Process focus uses management and improvement as an engine for growth and success. The processes in Six Sigma are documented, communicated, measured, and redefined on an ongoing basis. Processes are also designed and redesigned at intervals to stay current with customer and business needs.

- Proactive management anticipates problems and changes, applies facts and data, and questions assumptions about goals and how things are done.

- Boundaryless collaboration is seamless cooperation between internal groups and extended enterprise, including customers, suppliers, and supply chain partners.

- A drive for perfection and tolerance of failed experiments gives people in a Six Sigma organization the freedom to test new approaches while managing risks and learning from mistakes, thereby "raising the bar" of performance and customer satisfaction.

Six Sigma initiatives begin with a decision to change—specifically to learn and adopt methods that can improve performance of the organization. The depth of impact on the management processes and skills may vary, depending on how extensively the organization wants to apply the Six Sigma tools and the extent of the results. When looking at assessing the Six Sigma readiness of an organization, the following steps should be considered:

1. Assess the outlook and future path of the business for both short- and long-term, specifically in the areas of the clarity of the strategic course for the company, probability for meeting the financial and growth goals, and the ability of managing change.

2. Assess the current performance, such as current overall business results, the ability to understand and meet the customer's needs and the level of re-work and waste that exists in the current processes.

3. Review systems and capacity for change and improvement.

4. Summarize the assessment to determine if change is a critical business need based on the bottom line, culture or competitive needs, if the change is supported by senior management, and that existing improved systems and methods are capable of achieving the degree of change to keep a successful organization competitive.

## SIX SIGMA IMPLEMENTATION

Implementing Six Sigma involves the following steps:

1. Identify core processes and key customers and outputs of the core processes that can be applied to improve the understanding of the business.

2. Define customer requirements and identify key actions and challenges in strengthening the voice of the customer, specify output and service requirements of the customer and ways to better understand how customer needs link to the organization's strategy and priorities.

3. Measure current performance and identify the basic concepts in business process measurement, the basic steps in implementing customer and process-focused measures, and ways to effectively carry out data collection and sampling. This also includes types of defects and performance measures that are fundamental to the Six Sigma system.

4. Using Six Sigma process improvements, define, measure and analyze, and improve key business processes. The improvement process also focuses on identifying and eliminating the root cause as well as the basic tools of process improvement.

5. Using Six Sigma process design/redesign, define conditions that are essential to take on a process design or redesign project, and identify special tools and challenges that come into play during the design/redesign of a business process.

6. Expand and integrate the Six Sigma System and identify specific responsibilities and considerations for a process owner and ways

that the discipline of process management supports the Six Sigma system and long-term improvement.

The keys to successful Six Sigma implementation include:

- Tie Six Sigma efforts to business strategy and priorities. Show how projects and other activities link to customers, core processes, and competitiveness, where possible.

- Position Six Sigma as an improved way to manage today's business. Address the challenges of rapid change, intense competition, and increasingly demanding customers.

- Keep the message simple and clear. Make the core of the system and the organization's vision for Six Sigma accessible and meaningful to everyone.

- Develop one's own path to Six Sigma. Ensure the path or approach to Six Sigma is flexible and responsive to the organization.

- Focus on short-term results. Develop and push forward a plan that will make initial achievements realized within four to six months.

- Focus on long-term growth and development. Be ready for continuous improvement, and even redesign the Six Sigma processes as your organization progresses.

- Use the Six Sigma tools appropriately. Apply all the Six Sigma tools/methods in the right balance to maximize the results. Use the simplest tools that work and the use of complex tools should be carefully evaluated.

- Link customers, process, data, and innovation to build the Six Sigma system. Use measures and creativity to maximize value and performance to be at the competitive edge.

- Make senior management responsible and accountable. Demonstrate the Six Sigma project receives support from senior management and strengthen the importance of the initiative.

- Make learning an ongoing activity. Ensure ongoing efforts of looking outside the Six Sigma discipline for other disciplines that complement the existing tools.

Without question, there are costs associated with implementing Six Sigma. An entity must include the improvement opportunities presented in the business and the planned implementation to determine the pay-offs. Estimating potential benefits should include possible monetary gain from Six Sigma by evaluating the cost of rework, efficiency, or lost customers and the amount that the improvement opportunity will likely recover. If these cost savings are not enough to support the cost of implementation, then other approaches should be considered.

Performance management should allow the extended enterprise to act in a strategic manner in alignment with its mission and vision, using the overall knowledge gained. Acting on this newfound management cycle, the enterprise is better able to support its decisions and to monitor performance.

## SWOT (STRENGTH, WEAKNESSES, OPPORTUNITY, AND THREAT) ANALYSIS

*SWOT analysis* is a framework for analyzing the strengths, weaknesses, opportunities, and threats that an organization faces. It helps management focus on the strengths, minimize weaknesses, and take the greatest possible advantage of opportunities available. Analysis using the SWOT framework will help one to focus the activities into areas with the strongest and greatest opportunities, as well as being a decision-making aid. In general, the tool covers the following areas:

- Strengths:
    - Identify your advantages.
    - Identify areas that you do well.
    - Identify areas that other people view as your strengths.
    - Identify areas that you view as your strengths.
- Weaknesses:
    - Identify areas or activities that you view as area(s) that are not doing very well for the organization.
    - Identify areas or activities that you view as area(s) that you should avoid for the organization.
- Opportunities:
    - Identify where the good opportunities are for the organization.
    - Identify any interesting trends that you are aware of that would impact the organization.
    - Useful opportunities can come from changes in technology and markets on both broad and narrow scale, changes in government policy related to your field, changes in social patterns, population profiles, lifestyle changes, and local events.

- Threats:
    - Identify obstacles that you are facing.
    - Identify areas in which your competitors are doing something.
    - Identify any changes in job requirements or descriptions, and products or services.
    - Identify any changes in technology that may threaten the job or position.
    - Identify any cash flow or bad debts problems.

The process of utilizing the SWOT approach may include an internal analysis of strengths and weaknesses of the organization and an external analysis at the main points in the environmental analysis. It may also identify those points that pose threats or obstacles to performance and opportunities for the organization. It is an excellent fast tool for exploring the possibilities for initiating new programs. SWOTs can be performed by the individual administrator or in groups. However, group techniques have been noted to be particularly effective in providing structure, objectivity, clarity, and focus to discussions about strategy. The results of a SWOT analysis often reveal what needs to be done and puts problems into perspective.

SWOT analysis can be used for examination of an organization's internal strengths and weaknesses, and its environments, opportunities, and threats. It is a general tool designed to be used in the preliminary stages of decision making and as precursor to strategic planning in various kinds of applications. An understanding of the external factors, (including threats and opportunities) coupled with an internal examination of strengths and weaknesses assists in forming the vision of the future. Such foresight would translate into initiating competent programs or replacing redundant, irrelevant programs with innovative and relevant ones.

To be used most effectively, a SWOT analysis needs to be flexible. Situations may change with the passage of time, and an updated analysis should be made periodically to reflect the change.

## BUSINESS BALANCED SCORECARD PERFORMANCE MANAGEMENT TOOL

In the extended enterprise, there are four perspectives needed for a strategy roadmap:

1. Learning and growth
2. Internal business processes

**3.** Customer perspective

**4.** Financial performance

Customer perspective is the heart of an enterprises' strategy. It defines how growth is to be achieved, and the enterprise's value proposition defines the specific strategy to compete for new customers or to increase the share of existing customer business. For the customer, definition of the value proposition is the key to a stronger relationship with the enterprise. Business processes and activities that are internal to the organization need to be established to support delivery of the customer-value proposition. The learning and growth perspective represents the competencies, knowledge, technology, and climate needed to support the business processes and activities internally, as well as to deliver the promised value outcome to the customer. This will result in a better financial position.

If there is a significant change to the environment or in the customer-value proposition offered, the enterprise mission and values may be required to be reviewed and changed accordingly.

The balanced scorecard provides executives and managers a great deal of information just at one glance. It consists of a set of measures that give top managers a fast but comprehensive view of the business. The balanced scorecard includes financial measures that describe the results of actions already taken and hopefully will complement those with operational measures of the satisfaction of the customer, internal processes, and the organizational measures that are the drivers of future financial performance. In the extended enterprise environment, managers must be able to view performance in several areas simultaneously. The balanced scorecard allows enterprises to think of mission/strategies and to look at the business. In particular, it provides answers from four important perspectives:

**1.** How do we look to shareholders or stakeholders, made up of suppliers and partners (financial perspective)?

**2.** How do customers view our operations (customer perspective)?

**3.** What internal processes must we excel at to retain our business share (internal business perspective)?

**4.** How can we continue to improve and create value, making us better and more in demand by our customers, partners, suppliers, and so on (innovation and learning perspective)?

Each measure of a business balanced scorecard is lodged in a chain of cause-and-effect logic that connects the desired outcomes from the strategy with the drivers that will lead to the strategic outcomes. There is a need to describe the process for transforming intangible assets (i.e., employee efforts) into tangible customer and financial outcomes and provide all with a framework for describing and managing strategy in an extended enterprise. Outcomes should be established and contain a list of desirable outcomes of a mission. Desirable outcomes are satisfied shareholders, satisfied customers, effective processes, and a motivated and ready enterprise workforce.

The balanced scorecard places strategy and vision at the center of the items such as financial, customer, internal processes and learning and innovation. It proactively establishes consensus of goals among the people in an extended enterprise so that people will buy-in and adopt whatever behaviors and take whatever actions are necessary to arrive at these goals. The measures are designed to direct people in the extended enterprise toward the overall vision and assist or compel managers to focus on the handful of measures that are most critical. Senior management may know what the end result should be, but they cannot tell people exactly how to achieve that result, if only because the conditions in which the partners' people operate are constantly changing.

The methodology applies performance measures across a balanced scorecard perspective based on a department unit's progress on a business continuum as an example. The continuum could be structured in three phases, where each phase has a goal coupled with categories of complexity and elements to further define the measures, while the measures remain constant throughout the three phases.

*Phase 1*  Technology and process involves using the Internet internally and establishing a website. Technology implementation should be based on a reexamination and reengineering of core processes.

*Phase 2*  Access or transactions are allowed on core systems.

*Phase 3*  Core business processes are improved or the core processes are redesigned to create a seamless environment. The emphasis here is on business process improvement using technology as an enabler.

Measurement programs are designed to support the decisions made at different levels in the organization. However, scorecards are normally suited for executive-level decisions and convey business types of indicators, which key decision makers must address. Further, the scorecards should be tied to the reports used in managing the ongoing tasks of the program. As organizations have applied the balanced scorecard, it is recognized that the scorecard represents a fundamental change in the underlying assumptions about performance measurement.

The performance and goals are based on the department's level of maturity along the continuum. As the business continuum advances beyond the customary perceptions, a new continuum evolves from a relatively narrow focus capability for core processes to a tightly integrated shared data environment. The continuum not only allows access but also identifies areas requiring improvement and redefines the core processes.

Current businesses in the extended enterprise are normally covered by agreements between two organizations for integration, coordination, measurement, and awareness. They measure intercompany cross-functional processes using measures that are both functional and financial in nature. The balanced scorecard can be a vital tool for agreement not only between two organizations but also among partners within extended enterprises.

## NOTE

1. Per S. Pande, Robert P. Neuman, and Roland R. Cavanagh, *The Six Sigma Way: How GE, Motorola, and Other Top Companies Are Honing Their Performance* (New York: McGraw-Hill, 2000).

# APPENDIX C

# ORGANIZATIONAL STRUCTURE EVOLUTION: CORE VERSUS CENTRAL

In today's hectic world of Net-centric communications and multiple information flows, many of the conventional models of business operations can no longer deliver the needed results. These changes to their environment have forced enterprises to reexamine the way they structure themselves. A similar evaluation took place among organizations in the 1970s and again in the 1980s. These earlier changes featured organizations moving from total command-and-control structures to the concept of business units. As the business unit concept exhausted its usefulness, there was a movement to share services. Today, enterprises are focusing themselves as never before on capabilities—core competencies and value rather than on mere business structures. Of course, the ability to compete in a knowledge-based economy is driving this revolution as well. Organizations now ask themselves, "What more can be done with what we have?" This contrasts with merely asking if a unit or service should be kept.

Today, the organizational structure debate focuses on core versus central organization. What this means is that enterprises are focusing on those activities and resources that add value to the enterprise, and where they consider themselves to match or set world-class levels of performance. They distribute core activities on a global basis, to the areas of their activities where they have a world-class advantage. This focus on core activities has, at its root, governance, the need for effective value creation, the demands of customer focus, and the need to establish a unique identity. Enterprises then outsource or co-source all the rest of the services that do not fit into this core. There is no longer focus on centralized services.

Of course, what is core to one entity may not be core to another. However, typically a core-focused enterprise will look to transfer those services it sees as transaction-based to its extended partners, who operate outside the core of the enterprise. The culture, mission, and goals of the enterprise will also have an impact on what drives or determines what is viewed as core. Each enterprise must also ask itself some questions in deciding its approach to evaluate this process. Increased governance capabilities, strategic competitive advantage, and economies of scale are just a few of the issues that enterprises may wish to address when determining whether a function can be viewed as core. In a centralized organization, Exhibit C.1, the rigid structure of the entity is cause for concern. Speed to market and efficiency are secondary to ensuring a central command.

For example, the human resources element of many organizations is one of the few departments still part of the "central" part of organizations. However, even this has begun to be viewed as noncore with some entities and is beginning to be pushed outside. Additionally, most enterprises understand that they will never be world class within their HR department activities, nor do they want to—as most of it is not part of their core. What is part of their core are those activities that impact on their focus on strategy, their leadership development capabilities, and allocation of key personnel. Other common HR activities, such as payroll, benefits administration, recruiting, and training, are not part of the

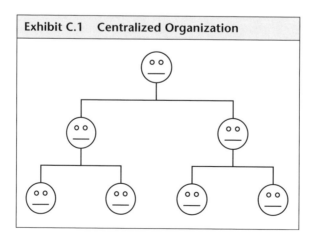

**Exhibit C.1    Centralized Organization**

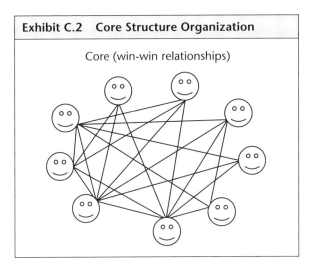

Exhibit C.2    Core Structure Organization

Core (win-win relationships)

core, so they can be outsourced or extended to partners who are able to provide world-class best practice in these activities, where these elements are a core part of their separate enterprise.

Another example deals with the IT element in today's enterprises. Traditionally, IT was viewed as a distinct part of the "central" part of enterprises. It operated and charged units whether they used the services or not. As time has passed, many organizations have moved to a shared services approach to the utilization of IT, and away from the central approach. This has allowed IT to move from a cost center to a quasi profit center, but some of the cores versus central issues remain. As with the HR example previously mentioned, an organization must ask itself whether IT operations are part of its core competency. Does the operation of IT impact the strategy, leadership, vision, and competency of the enterprise? If not, then these IT operations such as programming help desk, training, network operations, and maintenance could be outsourced to a world class partner—thus extending the enterprise.

In a core-structured organization, Exhibit C.2, the focus is on achieving win-win relationships. Whoever can get the job done best does it, and aims to best satisfy the customer. All groups are working together for either unified or congruent goals.

In both the examples given, the entities are described as practicing the centerless organizational structure. The structures of these enterprises are flat, with a network of interdependent business units and strategic alliances, partners, and so on. The flow is not up and down but in whatever direction is most effective for the enterprise to accomplish its objectives. As shown in Exhibit C.3, the core replaces the central focus of

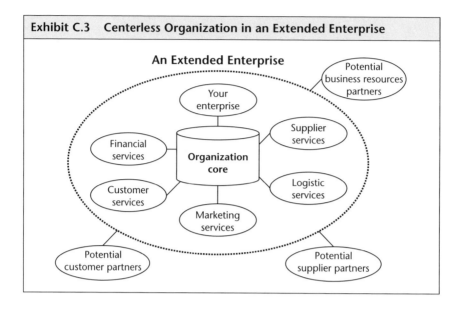

Exhibit C.3    Centerless Organization in an Extended Enterprise

entities, and the shift moves to shared services as well as to partners, suppliers, and potential customers outside of the enterprise, thus establishing fully what is described by the extended enterprise concept.

As shown in Exhibit C.3, everything operates without a center, and the core drives everything. If something is not part of the core competency of an enterprise, then it is outsourced or co-sourced to another world-class partner. The core concept has ramifications on the requirements for boards of director responsibilities as well. The board will interact at more frequent intervals with the core of the enterprise. It acquires a greater role in the decision making. As well, it may be that the core will be increasingly responsible for providing knowledge to the board as opposed to mere information. As organizations embrace the extended enterprise concept, the board will move to be a more proactive partner in the decision-making process.

# APPENDIX D

# FRAMEWORK AND QUALITY AWARDS

Enterprise objectives can be readily extended in scope by matching them with business excellence models on quality management. There are a number of business quality excellence and performance management models that can be adapted to governance measurement criteria. Four are most commonly accepted:

1. Malcolm Baldrige quality framework in the United States
2. Deming Prize in Japan
3. EFQM model for excellence in the European Union
4. ISO 9000-2000, which has global application, especially in the manufacturing environment

## MALCOLM BALDRIGE NATIONAL QUALITY AWARD FRAMEWORK

One such globally respected set of governance criteria is the Malcolm Baldrige National Quality Framework of the United States. Even though it is positioned as a performance measurement criterion, it can be easily utilized as a governance structure for the extended enterprise. The director of the Baldrige National Quality Criteria Framework, Harry S. Hertz, said to all U.S. CEOs that "Whether your business challenges are e-commerce and the Internet economy, globalization, rapid innovation, outsourcing, supply chain management, cost reduction or just maintaining your competitive advantage, the Baldrige Criteria can help you address them."

## Core Values and Concepts

The Baldrige Criteria are built on the following set of interrelated core values and concepts:

- *Visionary leadership.* An organization's senior leaders should set directions and create a customer focus, clear and visible values, and high expectations. The directions, values, and expectations should balance the needs of all stakeholders.

- *Customer-driven excellence.* Value and satisfaction may be influenced by many factors throughout the customers' overall purchase, ownership, and service experiences. These factors include the organization's relationship with customers that help build trust, confidence, and loyalty.

- *Organizational and personal learning.* Getting to the highest levels of business performance means a well-executed approach to organizational and personal learning. Organizational learning includes both continuous improvement of existing approaches and adaptation to change, leading to new goals and/or approaches.

- *Valuing employees and partners.* An entity's success will depend more and more on the knowledge, skills, creativity, and motivation of its employees and partners.

- *Agility.* Businesses face ever-shorter cycles for the introduction of new/improved products and services, as well as for faster and more flexible response to customers.

- *Focus on the future*. Pursuit of sustainable growth and market leadership requires a strong future orientation and a willingness to make long-term commitments to key stakeholders—customers, employees, suppliers and partners, stockholders, the public, and the community.

- *Managing for innovation*. Innovation means making meaningful change to improve an organization's products, services, and processes and to create new value for the organization's stakeholders.

- *Management by fact.* Organizations depend on the measurement and analysis of performance. Such measurements should derive from business needs and strategy, and they should provide critical data and information about key processes, outputs, and results.

- *Public responsibility and citizenship.* An organization's leaders should stress its responsibilities to the public and the need to practice good citizenship.
- *Focus on results and creating value.* An entity's performance measurements need to focus on key results.
- *Systems perspective.* Successful management of overall performance requires organization-specific synthesis and alignment.

## Criteria for Performance Excellence Framework

The core values and concepts are embodied in seven categories, as listed and depicted in Exhibit D.1. They are:

1. Leadership
2. Strategic planning
3. Customer and market focus
4. Information and analysis
5. Human resource focus
6. Process management
7. Business results

The criteria for the Baldrige National Quality Award Program are based on assessing a set of interrelated core values and concepts that are embedded beliefs and behaviors found in many of the most high-performing organizations. They are the foundation for integrating key business requirements within a results-oriented framework that creates a basis for action and feedback. The framework for assessment is divided into three main areas of concentration: organizational profile, system, and information and analysis.

## Organizational Profile

This preface sets the context for assessing the way an enterprise operates. It includes the environment, key working relationships, and organizational/strategic challenges. It serves as a guide for evaluating the enterprise performance management system.

## System

This system supports the organizational profile and is composed of six criteria that define the organization, its operations, and its results. These

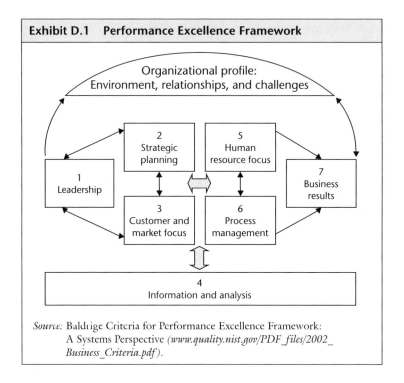

**Exhibit D.1    Performance Excellence Framework**

Organizational profile:
Environment, relationships, and challenges

2 Strategic planning

5 Human resource focus

1 Leadership

7 Business results

3 Customer and market focus

6 Process management

4 Information and analysis

*Source:* Baldrige Criteria for Performance Excellence Framework: A Systems Perspective *(www.quality.nist.gov/PDF_files/2002_Business_Criteria.pdf)*.

six categories are grouped into two pillars, namely leadership and results. The leadership pillar includes evaluation of leadership, strategic planning, and customer and market focus criteria. The results pillar includes consideration of human resource focus, process management, and business results.

The linkage between the leadership pillar and the results pillar is two-way communication, which is critical to the enterprise's success. It indicates the importance of feedback in an effective performance management system in addition to a direct relationship between leadership and implementing and delivering business results. The specific assessment criteria used by the Baldrige Award to obtain a perspective of enterprise-wide alignment can best be described as follows:

- *Leadership.* Examining how the extended enterprise's senior leaders address values, directions, and performance expectations, as well as focusing on customers and other stakeholders, empowerment, innovation, and learning. It also examines how the enterprise addresses its responsibilities to the public and supports its key communities. The leadership criterion drives and impacts the direction of both the strategic planning and customer and market focus.

- **Strategic planning.** Examining how the enterprise develops strategic objectives and action plans, the procedures for selection of strategic objectives, the deployment of action plans, enhancement of competitive position, and overall performance.

- **Customer and market focus.** Examining how the enterprise determines requirements, expectations, and preferences of customers and markets, as well as how to build relationships with customers. It also determines key factors that would lead to customer acquisition, satisfaction, and retention, and to business expansion. It also evaluates how senior leaders within the enterprise set directions and create a customer focus with clear visible values and high expectations. The leaders should ensure the creation of strategies, systems, and methods for achieving excellence, including stimulating innovation and building knowledge and capabilities.

- **Human resource focus.** Describing how the enterprise motivates and enables employees to develop and utilize their full potential in alignment with the organization's overall objectives and action plan. It assesses various efforts to build and maintain a work environment and a climate conducive to performance excellence and personal and organizational growth.

- **Process management.** Examining key aspects of the enterprise's process management, including customer-focused design, product and service delivery, key business and support processes.

- **Business results.** Examining the organization's performance, how it compares to its competitors, and how it achieves improvement in key business areas, such as customer satisfaction, product and service performance, financial and marketplace performance, human resources results, and operational performance

## Information and Analysis

Within each enterprise is stored a wealth of information, as well as the people with the knowledge of what to do with it. This knowledge collectively amounts to the brain center of the enterprise, and its use is central in making use of the entity's information and ensuring its availability and quality. IT plays a key role in storing this information and enabling it to be extracted and reported.

## DEMING AWARD

The Deming Prize was introduced in 1951 by the Japanese Union of Scientists and Engineers (JUSE) to honor W. Edwards Deming and drive the implementation of quality control. The Deming Prize provides a checklist for policies, organization, information, standardization, quality assurance, maintenance, improvement, effects, and future plans. It also provides a checklist for evaluating executive performance, which includes coverage of leadership understanding, policies on leadership approach, organization for leadership deployment, human resources, and implementation from a leadership deployment perspective.

The categories of the Deming Prize are:

- The Deming Prize for Individuals who have made outstanding contributions to the study
- The Deming Application Prize
- The Quality Control Award for Operations Business Units

### Deming Application Prize[1]

*The Deming Application Prize is an annual award presented to a company that has achieved distinctive performance improvements through the application of TQM. Regardless of the types of industries, any organization can apply for the Prize, be it public or private, large or small, or domestic or overseas. Provided that a division of a company manages its business autonomously, the division may apply for the Prize separately from the company. Companies or divisions of companies that apply for the Prize (applicant companies hereafter) receive the examination by the Deming Application Prize Subcommittee (the Subcommittee hereafter). Based on the results of the Subcommittee's examination, the Deming Prize Committee selects the winners.*

*There is no limit to the number of potential recipients of the Prize each year. All organizations that score the passing points or higher upon examination will be awarded the Deming Application Prize.*

*In the event that a passing point score has not been attained by the applicant, final judgment is reserved, and unless withdrawal is requested by the applicant, the status is considered as 'continued examination.' Subsequent examinations are limited to twice during the next three years. Subsequent examinations will focus on what was highlighted at the previous examination and what has changed since then. The applicant is recognized as having passed the examination when it has sufficiently improved upon the previously noted issues and has successfully achieved the necessary levels.*

### Eligibility

*The Deming Application Prize is given to an applicant company that effectively practices TQM suitable to its management principles, type of industry, and business scope. More specifically, the following three viewpoints are used for the examination to determine whether or not the applicant should be awarded the Prize:*

1. *Reflecting its management principles, type of industry, business scope, and business environment, the applicant has established challenging and customer-oriented business objectives and strategies under its clear management leadership.*

2. *TQM has been implemented properly to achieve business objectives and strategies as mentioned in Item 1 above.*

3. *As an outcome of Item 2, the outstanding results have been obtained for business objectives and strategies as stated in Item 1.*

## EUROPEAN FOUNDATION FOR QUALITY (EFQM) FRAMEWORK

Another well-respected framework is the EFQM framework. The EFQM Excellence Model is a nonprescriptive framework based on eight criteria and essentials of excellence. The model, recognizing there are many approaches to achieving sustainable excellence in all aspects of performance, is based on the premise that excellent results with respect to performance, customers, people, and society are achieved through partnerships, resources, and processes. The Eight Essentials of Excellence and their ensuing benefits are explained in the following paragraphs.

## Results Orientation

Excellence is dependent on balancing and satisfying the needs of all relevant stakeholders (this includes the people employed, customers, suppliers, and society in general as well as those with financial interests in the organization). Benefits include:

- Adding value for stakeholders
- Sustainable long-term success
- Mutually beneficial relationships
- Relevant measures, including leading indicators

## Customer Focus

The customer is the final arbiter of product and service quality, and customer loyalty, retention, and market share gains are best optimized through a clear focus on the needs of current and potential customers. Benefits include:

- Clear understanding of how to deliver value
- Market share gain
- Long-term success

## Leadership and Constancy of Purpose

The behavior of an organization's leaders creates a clarity and unity of purpose within the organization and an environment in which the organization and its people can excel. Benefits include:

- Maximized people commitment and effectiveness
- Clear sense of direction
- Marketplace respect
- All activities aligned and deployed in a structured way

## Management by Processes and Facts

Organizations perform more effectively when all interrelated activities are understood and systematically managed, and decisions concerning current operations are planned. Improvements are made using reliable information that includes stakeholder perceptions. Benefits include:

- Focus on desired outcomes
- Maximized use of people and resources
- Consistency of outcomes
- Fact-based management setting realistic goals and direction

## People Development and Involvement

The full potential of an organization's people is best released through shared values and a culture of trust and empowerment, which encourages the involvement of everyone. Benefits include:

- Positive attitude and morale
- Positive organizational recruitment and retention

- Effective knowledge sharing
- Learning and skill development opportunities

### Continuous Learning, Innovation, and Improvement

Organizational performance is maximized when it is based on the management and sharing of knowledge within a culture of continuous learning, innovation, and improvement. Benefits include:

- Organizational agility
- Cost reduction
- Performance optimization

### Partnership Development

An organization works more effectively when it has mutually beneficial relationships, built on trust, sharing of knowledge, and integration with its partners. Benefits include:

- Value creation for all parties
- Competitive advantage
- Synergy related to costs and resources

### Public Responsibility

Adopting an ethical approach and exceeding the expectations and regulations of the community at large best serve the long-term interest of the organization and its people. Benefits include:

- Enhanced credibility and organizational value
- Public awareness, trust, and confidence

### ISO 9000-2000

Another global framework is that of ISO 9000-2000. It is focused on quality and consists of a set of eight quality-management principles.

1. **Focus on Your Customers.** Organizations rely on customers. Therefore:
   - Organizations must understand customer needs.
   - Organizations must meet customer requirements.
   - Organizations must exceed customer expectations.

2. **Provide Leadership.** Organizations rely on leaders. Therefore:
   - Leaders must establish a unity of purpose and set the direction the organization should take.
   - Leaders must create an environment that encourages people to achieve the organization's objectives.

3. **Involve Your People.** Organizations rely on people. Therefore:
   - Organizations must encourage the involvement of people at all levels.
   - Organizations must help people to develop and use their abilities.

4. **Use a Process Approach.** Organizations are more efficient and effective when they use a process approach. Therefore:
   - Organizations must use a process approach to manage activities and related resources.

5. **Take a Systems Approach.** Organizations are more efficient and effective when they use a systems approach. Therefore:
   - Organizations must identify interrelated processes and treat them as a system.
   - Organizations must use a systems approach to manage their interrelated processes.

6. **Encourage Continual Improvement.** Organizations are more efficient and effective when they continually try to improve. Therefore:
   - Organizations must make a permanent commitment to continually improve their overall performance.

7. **Get the Facts Before You Decide.** Organizations perform better when their decisions are based on facts. Therefore:
   - Organizations must base decisions on the analysis of factual information and data.

8. **Work with Your Suppliers.** Organizations depend on their suppliers to help them create value. Therefore:
   - Organizations must maintain a mutually beneficial relationship with their suppliers.

## NOTE

1. The W. Edwards Deming Institute: *www.deming.org/demingprize/demingapplication.html* and *www.deming.org/demingprize/prizeinfo.html*.

# ──────── APPENDIX E ────────

# BUSINESS REFERENCE MODEL

When extended enterprises look to transform their governance system to one that is customer oriented and world-class core-competence relationship-based, they really should be looking to develop a business-based reference model for enterprisewide improvement. This might assist with analysis and identification of overlapping investments, gaps, and potential opportunities for collaboration within and across extended enterprises.

This business reference model is intended for use in analyzing investment in IT and other assets. It could also assist in future development of a broader architecture for a performance reporting/management system. The approach could define and communicate, for all interested stakeholders, a high-level view of how—in business terms— the extended enterprise can achieve its mission. Also, users identify how and where processes are being supported, where there are opportunities to reduce redundancies, and how to build more cost-effective solutions in the future.

As an example, the U.S. federal government has developed, for purposes of defining and communicating for all interested stakeholders, a high-level view of how—in business terms—it plans to achieve its various missions. It enables users to identify how processes are being supported, where they are being supported, where there are opportunities to reduce redundancies, and how to build more cost-effective solutions in the future. It contains three business areas, and each is differentiated by the service being provided. The model is organized and structured along three guiding principles; citizen (customer) focused, results oriented, and market based.

As with extended enterprises in the private market, there were some common reasons why the U.S. government felt it was necessary to develop this model, including:

- Simplifying delivery of services
- Eliminating waste and unnecessary layers of management
- Easily locating and using information
- Simplifying the business process and reducing costs through integration
- Streamlining operations
- The need to extend out to the customer, the citizen

The lines of business are the cornerstone of defining the services of the federal government and how it delivers these services to the public and/or other federal agencies. As shown in Exhibit E.1, four business areas provide a high-level view of the types of operations the U.S. federal government performs:

1. **Services for Citizens.** Describes the mission and purpose of the U.S. government in terms of the services it provides both to and on behalf of the American citizen. It includes the delivery of citizen-focused, public, and collective goods and/or benefits as a service and/or obligation of the federal government to the benefit and protection of the nation's general population.

2. **Mode of Delivery.** Describes the mechanisms the government uses to achieve the purpose of government, or its services to citizens. It includes financial vehicles, direct government delivery, and indirect government delivery.

3. **Support Delivery of Services.** Aids the cause, policies, and interests that facilitate the federal government's delivery of its services, both to citizens and other federal agencies.

4. **Management of Government Resources.** Refers to the back-office support activities that must be performed for the federal government to operate. This business area includes inter- and intra-agency internal operations. Whereas most agencies' back-office activities support their citizen-focused lines of business, *intra-agency,* there are agencies that provide services for or leverage services from other federal agencies. These activities are distinguished within the *interagency* internal operations business area.

The value in having a business reference model for any extended enterprise relationship is that it facilitates efforts so all that are involved can see easily see and analyze investment in IT and other assets. It can

**Exhibit E.1    U.S. Federal Enterprise Architecture Business Reference Model (BRM) Version 2.0**

**Services for Citizens**

Defense and National Security
Homeland Security
Intelligence Operations
Law Enforcement
International Affairs and Commerce
Litigation and Judicial Activities
Correctional Activities

Education
Energy
Health
Transportation
Income Security

Environmental Management
Natural Resources
Disaster Management
Community and Social Services
Economic Development
Workforce Management
General Science and Innovation

**Mode of Delivery**

Government Service Delivery
Direct Services for Citizens
Knowledge Creation and Mgmt
Public Goods Creation and Mgmt
Regulatory Compliance and Enforcement

Financial Vehicles
Federal Financial Assistance
Credit and Insurance
Transfers to States and Local Governments

**Support Delivery of Services**

Legislative Relations
Public Affairs
Regulatory Development
Planning and Resource Allocation

General Government

Controls and Oversight
Revenue Collection
Internal Risk Mgmt and Mitigation

**Management of Government Resources**

Supply Chain Management
Human Resource Management

Financial Management

Administrative Management
Information and Technology Mgmt

*Source:* U.S. Federal Enterprise Architecture Program Management Office, June 2003.

also assist in future development of a broader architecture for a performance reporting/management system. The approach could define and communicate, for all interested stakeholders, a high-level view of how—in business terms—the extended enterprise can achieve its mission. Also, users identify how and where processes are being supported, where there are opportunities to reduce redundancies, and how to build more cost-effective solutions in the future.

One of the side benefits that can be discerned by implementing this approach is to enable a full mapping of systems and resources used for an extended enterprise environment. From there it will be fairly easy to determine overlaps and efficiencies, if any.

Of course, having a business reference model is only the first step in the identification process of better understanding the partners involved in the extended enterprise environment. From here, work must proceed on the development and implementation of a performance model, which will provide common measures throughout the extended enterprise. This model will provide common measures for valuing operations of the extended enterprise. This approach is detailed in Appendix B, "Performance Reference Models."

Exhibit E.2 is a sample U.S. federal government business reference model for 24 agencies or departments. This is not an extended enterprise model but does show some similar features as an extended enterprise. An

## Exhibit E.2   U.S. Agency Mappings

Services to Citizens Business Area
Analytical Summary
Average Number of Agencies per Subfunction is 5
Average Number of Agencies per Line of Business is 10
Average Number of Lines of Business per Agency is 10
Average Number of Subfunctions per Agency is 19

| Business Area | Subfunction | USAID | USDA | Commerce | Education | Energy | HHS | HUD | DoI | DoJ | DoL | State | Transportation | Treasury | EPA | FEMA | GSA | NARA | NASA | NSF | NRC | OPM | SBA | SSA | VA | Number of agencies |
|---|---|---|---|---|---|---|---|---|---|---|---|---|---|---|---|---|---|---|---|---|---|---|---|---|---|---|
| Public asset management | Cultural archives and artifacts | | | | | | | | | | | | | | | | | | | | | | | | | 0 |
| | Public funds | | | | | | X | | | | | | | X | | | X | | | | | X | | | | 4 |
| | Public facilities | | X | X | | X | X | X | X | | | X | X | X | X | | X | X | | | | | | | | 12 |
| | Public records/data management | | | X | | | | | X | | | | | X | X | X | X | X | | X | | | | | X | 9 |
| Defense and national security operations | Antiterrorism | | | | | X | | | | X | | X | X | X | X | X | X | | | | | | | | | 8 |
| | Border control | X | X | | | | | | | X | | X | X | X | | | | | | | | | | | X | 7 |
| | Intelligence gathering | | | | | | | | | X | | X | X | | | | | | | | | | | | | 3 |
| | Military operations | | | | | | | | | | | | X | | | | | | | | | | | | | 1 |
| | Weapons control | | | X | | X | | | | X | | X | | | | | | | X | | | | | | | 5 |
| Public health | Illness prevention | X | | | | | X | | | | | | | | | | | | | | | X | | | X | 4 |
| | Immunization management | X | | | | | X | | | | | | | | | | | | | | | | | | X | 3 |
| | Public health monitoring | X | X | X | | | X | | | | | | | X | | X | | | | | | | | | | 6 |
| Energy management | Energy distribution | | | | | X | | | | | | X | | | | | | | | | | | | | | 2 |
| | Energy production | | | | | X | | | | | | X | | | | | | | | | | | | | | 2 |
| | Energy resource management | | X | | | | | | | | | X | | X | | | X | | | | | | | | | 4 |
| Domestic economy | Business/industry development | X | X | X | | | | | | | X | X | X | X | X | | X | | X | | | | X | | | 11 |
| | Monetary control | | | | | | | X | | | | | | X | X | | | | | | | | | | | 3 |
| Social services | Burial services | | | | | | | | | | | | | | | | | | | | | | | | | 0 |
| | Community development | | X | X | | | | X | X | | | | | X | X | X | | X | | | | | X | | | 9 |
| | Food assistance | | X | | | | | | | | | | | | | | | | | | | | | | | 1 |
| | Housing benefits | | | | | | | X | X | | | | | | | | X | | | | | | | | | 3 |
| | Medical services | | | | | | X | | | | | | | | | | X | | | | | | | | X | 3 |
| | Monetary benefits | | | | X | X | | | | | X | X | | | | | X | | | | | | | X | X | 7 |
| Marketable asset management | Financial asset management | | | X | | | | | X | | | | | X | | | | | | | | | | | | 3 |
| | Personal property management | | | X | | | | | | X | | | | X | X | | X | | | | | | | | | 5 |
| | Real property management | | | X | | | | | X | | | | | X | | | X | | | | | | | | | 4 |
| Diplomacy and foreign relations | Conflict resolution | X | | | | | | | | | | X | | | | | | | | | | | | | | 2 |
| | Foreign socioeconomic and political development | X | X | X | | | | | | | | X | | X | X | | | | | | | | | X | | 7 |
| | Treaties and agreements | X | | X | | | | | | | | X | | X | X | | X | | | | | | | X | | 7 |
| Disaster management | Disaster monitoring and prediction | X | | X | | | | X | | | | X | | X | X | X | | | X | | | | | | | 8 |
| | Disaster preparedness/planning | X | | X | X | | X | X | | | | X | | X | X | X | X | X | | | | | | | | 11 |
| | Disaster repair and restore | X | X | X | X | | X | | | | | X | | X | X | X | X | X | | | | | | | | 11 |
| | Emergency response | X | | X | X | | X | | | | | X | | X | X | X | X | X | | | | | | | | 10 |
| Education | External training and education | X | | X | X | X | X | X | X | X | X | X | | X | X | X | X | X | X | | | X | X | X | X | 20 |
| | Advising and consulting | X | X | X | | | | | | X | X | X | | X | X | X | X | X | | | | X | X | | | 13 |
| | Promote education | X | | | X | | | | | | | | | | | | | | | | | | | | | 2 |
| Research and development and science | Data and statistics development | | | X | X | X | | X | | X | X | X | | X | X | X | X | X | | | | | | X | X | 14 |
| | Scientific research and development | X | X | X | | X | X | | X | | | | | X | X | | | | X | X | | | | | | 10 |
| | Socioeconomic research and development | X | | X | | | | | | X | X | X | | X | X | X | | | | | | | | X | | 9 |
| | Technology research and development | | | X | X | X | | | X | X | | X | | X | X | | | | X | X | X | | | | | 11 |
| Transportation | Air traffic control | | | | | | | | | | | | X | | | | | | | | | | | | | 1 |
| | Land transportation | | X | | | | | | X | | | | X | | X | | X | | | | | | | | | 5 |
| | Maritime transportation | | | | | | | | X | | | | X | | | | | | | | | | | | | 2 |
| | Space operations | | | | | | | | | | | | X | | | | | | | | | | | | | 1 |
| Workforce management | Job creation | | X | | | | | | | X | X | | X | | | | | | | | | X | | | | 5 |
| | Labor rights management | | | | | | | | | X | X | X | | | | | X | | | | | | | | | 4 |
| | Worker safety | | | | | | | | | X | | | X | | X | | X | | | | | | | | | 4 |
| Recreation and natural resources | Conservation planning | | X | X | | | | | X | | | | | | X | | X | | | | | | | | | 5 |
| | Land and monument management | | X | X | | | | | X | | | | | | X | | X | | | | | | | | | 5 |
| | Tourism management | | | X | | | | | X | | | | | X | X | X | X | | | | | | | | | 6 |
| Insurance | Insurance issuing | | X | | | | | X | | | | | | X | | X | | | | | | X | X | X | X | 8 |
| | Insurance services | | X | | | | | X | | | | | | X | | X | | | | | | X | X | X | X | 8 |
| Consumer safety | Firearms and explosives safety | | | | | | | | | | | | | X | X | | | | | | | | | | | 2 |
| | Antitrust control | | | X | | | | | | | | | | X | | | | | | | | | | | | 2 |
| | Consumer products quality assurance | | X | X | | | X | | X | | | | | X | X | X | X | | | | | | | | | 8 |
| | Monetary protection | | | | | | | | | | | | | X | | | | | | | | | | | | 1 |
| Trade | Export promotion | X | X | X | | | | | | | | | | X | | | | | | | | X | X | | | 6 |
| | Merchandise inspection | | X | X | | | | | | X | | | | X | X | X | | | | | | | | | | 6 |
| | Tariff/quotas monitoring | | | X | | | | | | | | | | X | X | X | | | | | | | | | | 4 |

*Source:* U.S. Federal Enterprise Architecture Program Management Office, 2002.

approach such as this should be taken when determining what activities each partner is undertaking and what, if any, resources and or systems are being utilized. This approach can prove invaluable to ensure minimal overlap and proper alignment is occurring.

An additional example for maturity-level evaluation of governance criteria is Exhibit E.3. This is an architecture criteria example for the U.S. federal government's 24 agencies. Value, change, and leadership could be evaluated in the near future.

**Exhibit E.3    GAO Evaluated Maturity Model of Enterprise Architecture of Federal Agencies**

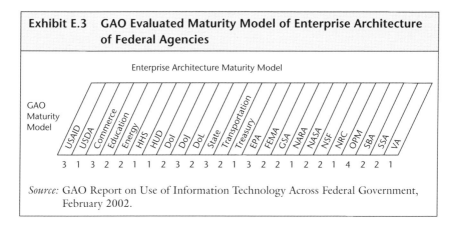

*Source:* GAO Report on Use of Information Technology Across Federal Government, February 2002.

# APPENDIX F

# KNOWLEDGE WORK, KNOWLEDGE MANAGEMENT, AND KNOWLEDGE PORTAL

## WHAT IS A KNOWLEDGE PORTAL?

In today's extended enterprise environment, many organizations are implementing knowledge portals for supporting knowledge work. *Knowledge portals* represent a combination of technologies and practices that serve key knowledge work tasks. Knowledge portals can serve as an ideal knowledge management tool where employees can share a wealth of corporate know-how.

Portals are valuable to users when they simplify complex information and when the information is context specific, provides useful services, and/or fosters collaboration and community building.

*Knowledge portal* is an approach to harvesting information from various sources using a single-point-access software system such as the Internet and Web browsers. In this role, the Web browser acts as a single-point-access of data from sources such as legacy database management and reporting systems, client-server networks, unrelated Internet and intranet Web sites, and perhaps syndicated services. In essence, Web browsers provide easy and timely access to information and support communities of knowledge workers who share common goals. In short, one can obtain virtually unlimited information that is available through the portals.

People frequently view portals as databases containing all the information that can be made available for user searches and have encountered inefficiency in searching for information as well as being overwhelmed with information from searches. A fundamental motivation for knowledge portals is to make knowledge works more productive. To achieve knowledge sharing, these portals must be properly designed, focusing on function and content. In essence, they need to change and adapt as the organization does.

## PORTAL DESIGN FOR THE EXTENDED ENTERPRISE

The key to a knowledge portal is to leverage on *knowledge management* and separate the management of *content* from *design*.

### Knowledge Management

The notion of knowledge management can assist development of synergy between the data and information process capacity of information technologies and the innovative and creative ways to share and benefit from enterprise knowledge. It can be viewed as a strategic process that promotes an integrated approach to identifying, managing, and sharing the enterprise's information assets. It captures the ways an organization integrates its information assets with the processes and policies that govern the exploitation of intellectual assets.

The concept of knowledge management may perhaps be best defined from how people utilize the knowledge and what people in the knowledge management fields are doing. In the e-business and extended enterprise environment, knowledge management can be defined into an information technology (IT) track and a people track. Furthermore, each individual track can be viewed at the organizational and individual level. For example, IT track knowledge management focuses on the management of information where knowledge is identified as objects that can be identified and handled in an information system. At the organizational level, the focus in research and practice is on the organization such as for reengineers and strategists. At the individual level, the focus is for specialists. For the people track, however, knowledge management focuses on the management of people. The primary involvement is in the areas of assessing, changing, and improving people skills and/or behavior. Knowledge is identified as processes, which is a complex set of dynamic skills and know-how that is constantly changing. At the organization level, the focus is on organization theory; and at the individual level, the focus is on the art of creating value from intangible assets.

## Content Management System

A content management system stores content in a database separately from the templates that control its appearance so content can be updated or reused in various contexts without touching the templates. When content is changed in the database, it automatically changes it in as many places as it resides and is related on the site.

Content management provides the process of creating, using, storing, indexing, and retrieving unstructured information in the form of office documents such as MS Word, Excel, and so on, as well as images, project plans, and text documents. Content management's concern is with the workflows employed to create, as well as document, components. It often serves as the backbone of large Web sites and provides version control and site management facilities. A content directory contains multiple folders; each folder contains documents or links to Web pages. Content management for a portal does not usually involve the editing pages on the Web site but, rather, the organization of those pages into a content directory.

A content management system usually provides the following components:

- Document templates
- A scripting language and/or markup language
- Integration with a database

## Portal Design

Portals serve tasks performed by knowledge workers. Knowledge workers gather information relevant to a task, organize, search, and analyze it. They also synthesize solutions with respect to specific task goals and then share and distribute what has been learned to other knowledge workers. This involves gathering information relevant to the subject. References may also be sought to colleagues who might have useful expertise to share.

Knowledge portals must be:

- Designed for evolution. As the community grows, new members bring new interest and may pull the focus of the community in different direction.

- Built on the collective experience of community members, where only an insider can appreciate the issues at the heart of the domain, the knowledge that is important to share, the challenges and potential in emerging ideas and techniques.

- Developed as a Web of enduring relationships among members. There is no right beat for all communities, and the beat is likely to change as the community evolves.

In the extended enterprise, the focus for both IT and People tracks and levels are extended to outside the organization to business partners, suppliers, and outsourcers. Implementation of a core information repository in an extended enterprise is complex work. The design of a knowledge portal for the extended enterprise should focus on the following:

- Competing demands for scope, time cost, risk, and quality

- Stakeholders (partners) with different needs and expectations

- Identified requirements

A clear graphical representation should be provided for the design of a knowledge portal for an extended enterprise. The scope of an extended enterprise should be flexible to meet the dynamic environment changes. The knowledge portal should have the capability of handling this complexity and flexibility, as illustrated in Exhibit F.1. This suggests the provision of a core repository of information—referred to as a core knowledge portal for the extended enterprise and a logical web-based implementation is referred to as a knowledge portal. The web of knowledge workers should include but not be limited to knowledge workers within the enterprise and existing financial, customer, marketing, logistics, and supplier partners. Further, it should take into consideration the knowledge work for potential customer, business resource, and supplier partners. Ongoing and periodic monitoring systems over quality, cost, and time of the project should be implemented, and risk factors for legal compliance, technology, complexity, and cultural diversity should be identified and monitored.

The initial design of a knowledge portal could be based on strategy, input from knowledge designers, and individuals within the community that are given the empowerment. As the environment changes, strategy and information maintained in the database need to be reviewed and updated as appropriate. Exhibit F.2 depicts one such knowledge portal relationship. One can use the SWOT analysis to identify the strength, weakness, opportunities, and threats resulting from the change and its impact to the established strategy. Adjustments should be made to the

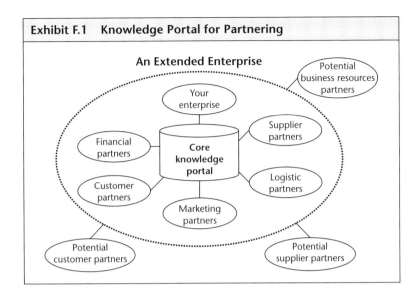

**Exhibit F.1    Knowledge Portal for Partnering**

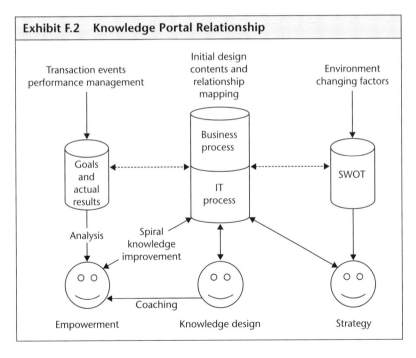

**Exhibit F.2    Knowledge Portal Relationship**

strategy, based on the change and input to the business process and IT process database.

Creating new knowledge is not simply a matter of mechanically processing objective information. New knowledge, most of the time, begins with the individual. Sometimes the knowledge of an individual is developed through coaching from the knowledge design; it may continue to be enhanced from shared information through business and IT processes and, thus, result in a spiral knowledge improvement condition.

Over time, performance results can be captured and analyzed against the goals and actual results. These results can be input into the business process and IT process and then relayed to the knowledge workers for further analysis and knowledge improvement and input to the business process and IT process database.

As stated by Ikujiro Nonaka in his article "The Knowledge Creating Company," there are three vital concepts that should be considered when developing a knowledge portal:[1]

1. *Metaphor.* A distinct method of perception created to provide a better understanding for individuals in different context and with different experiences without the need for analysis or generalization. Through metaphors, people put together what they know intuitively for the knowledge portal and begin to express what they know but have difficulty in articulating the knowledge. Although metaphor triggers the knowledge creation process, it alone is not sufficient.

2. *Analogy.* A more structured process established to reconcile any contradictions among individuals within the knowledge creation community and clarify the different ideas. The contradictions incorporated into metaphors are harmonized by analogy. In this respect, analogy is an intermediate step between intuition and logical thinking.

3. *Model creation.* Incorporates resolutions to any contradictions and concepts in a consistent and systematic logic stored in a database, thus making tacit knowledge into explicit.

Redundancy is also important for managing knowledge. It encourages frequent dialog and communication among employees and facilitates the transfer of tacit knowledge. Redundancy also promotes the sharing of explicit knowledge through the organization so that employees can internalize it. Building redundancy through the sharing of strategy among different functions or groups also helps employees understand the business from different perspectives and makes organizational knowledge easier to put into practice.

In summary, when building a knowledge portal, it must take into consideration knowledge management, content management, and portal design. Further, the design of a knowledge portal must take into consideration spiral knowledge improvement, input both internal and external to the enterprise, and the ability to capture knowledge from metaphor to analogy to model creation. Further redundancy should also be considered for knowledge management.

Enterprise architecture is one of a feasible strategic information assets base, which could be loaded on a knowledge portal for real time updating and sharing among IT related business strategists within an extended enterprise. Other strategic factors could also be handled on a knowledge portal for governance of an extended enterprise.

## NOTE

1. Nonaka Ikujiro, "The Knowledge-Creating Company," *Harvard Business Review on Knowledge Management* (Boston: Harvard Business School Press, 1998).

# APPENDIX G

# ENTERPRISE ARCHITECTURE PROCESSES AT DIFFERENT MATURITY LEVELS

Following the guidance of the U.S. CIO Council, the U.S. Department of Commerce developed an enterprisewide IT architecture (i.e., enterprise architecture plus a technical reference model and standard profiles). This step was taken in order to create a highly adaptive and enabling infrastructure that reduces integration complexity and lowers the total cost of ownership. The Commerce Department wanted to ensure continued progress building on previous efforts and to fully realize the benefits of its IT architecture.

To effectively structure management actions arising from analysis of the current architecture, it developed the IT enterprise architecture maturity model, as shown in Exhibit G.1. The objective of this model is to enhance the overall odds for success of the IT architecture by identifying weak areas. It can be looked at as a good first step within an extended enterprise to provide a defined path toward improvement. As an architecture approach matures, it should increase the benefits it offers the organization. The model delineates an evolutionary way to improve the overall process from commencement through to maturity, looking at any gaps. As can be seen, the types of questions or observations that are provided tend to become more concrete as the level of maturity increases.

| Characteristics | Level 0: No Architecture | Level 1: Initial | Level 2: Under Development | Level 3: Defined | Level 4: Managed | Level 5: Optimizing |
|---|---|---|---|---|---|---|
| **Business Linkage** | ■ No linkage to business strategies or business drivers. | ■ Minimal, or implicit, linkage to business strategies or business drivers. | ■ Explicit linkage to business strategies. | ■ Explicit linkage to business drivers and information requirements. | ■ Periodic re-examination of business drivers.<br>■ End-to-end process cycle time (business drivers to component definition) is measured. | ■ Process metrics for business linkage driven into requirements-gathering process improvements. |
| **Senior Management Involvement** | ■ Management resistant:<br>□ *We do not need it.*<br>□ *That will not work here.*<br>□ *Everything is fine the way it is.* | ■ Management becoming aware:<br>□ *What is architecture?*<br>□ *Why do we need it?* | ■ Management awareness of architecture effort:<br>□ *Much nodding of heads.*<br>□ *Some resistance to implications of having architecture.* | ■ Management awareness and support of architecture effort.<br>■ Management active support of architectural standards. | ■ Senior management reviews architecture process cycle times, variances. | ■ Management involvement in optimizing process improvements in architecture development and governance. |

**Exhibit G.1  Enterprise Architecture Processes at Different Maturity Levels** *(Continued)*

| Characteristics | Level 0: No Architecture | Level 1: Initial | Level 2: Under Development | Level 3: Defined | Level 4: Managed | Level 5: Optimizing |
|---|---|---|---|---|---|---|
| **Operating Unit Participation** | ■ No part of operating unit participation or involvement with IT architecture process. | ■ Operating unit resistant: <br> □ *We support the architecture process as long as it represents the standards we have already chosen.* <br> □ *Standards will only inhibit our ability to deliver business value.* | ■ Recognition that it is painful supporting too many kinds of technologies. <br> ■ Perhaps tired of distributing not fully developed or tested operating unit IT operations and support. | ■ Recognition that architectural standards can reduce integration complexity and enhance overall ability to operating unit IT to achieve business goals. <br> ■ Most of operating unit active participation in architecture definition. | ■ Entire operating unit active participation in architecture definition. | ■ Feedback from all elements of operating unit on architecture process is driving architecture process improvements. |
| **Architecture Process Definition** | ■ Not established. | ■ Ad hoc or informal form exists. <br> ■ Early draft form may exist. | ■ Architecture is being actively developed. <br> ■ Process definition not widely communicated. | ■ Defined and communicated to IT staff and business management with LOB or operating unit IT responsibilities. | ■ Architecture process is part of the culture, with strong linkages to other core IT and business processes. | ■ Concerted efforts to optimize and continuously improve architecture process definition. <br> ■ Modeling of proposed process changes before implementation. <br> *(continues)* |

**Exhibit G.1  Enterprise Architecture Processes at Different Maturity Levels** (*Continued*)

| Characteristics | Level 0: No Architecture | Level 1: Initial | Level 2: Under Development | Level 3: Defined | Level 4: Managed | Level 5: Optimizing |
|---|---|---|---|---|---|---|
| **Architecture Development** | ■ No architecture. | ■ Some processes, documentation and standards, established by a variety of ad hoc means. | ■ Architecture standards exist, but are not necessarily linked to overarching conceptual architecture.<br>■ Technical Reference Model and Standards Profile framework is established. | ■ Architecture standards development linked to business drivers via conceptual architecture of principles and best practices.<br>■ Partially completed Technical Reference Model and Standards Profile. | ■ Component architectures defined by appropriate de-jure and de-facto standards.<br>■ Fully developed Technical Reference Model and Standards Profile.<br>■ Architecture conformance measured by deployed systems. | ■ Same as Level 4, with process exceptions (standards waivers) improving architecture definition process. |

**Exhibit G.1 Enterprise Architecture Processes at Different Maturity Levels** *(Continued)*

| *Characteristics* | *Level 0: No Architecture* | *Level 1: Initial* | *Level 2: Under Development* | *Level 3: Defined* | *Level 4: Managed* | *Level 5: Optimizing* |
|---|---|---|---|---|---|---|
| **Governance** | ▪ None.<br>▪ Everyone does his or her own thing. | ▪ No explicit governance of architectural standards. | ▪ Explicit governance of a few architectural standards (e.g., desktops, database management systems).<br>▪ Variances may go undetected in the design and implementation phases. | ▪ Explicit governance of the bulk of IT investments.<br>▪ Formal processes for managing variances. | ▪ Explicit governance of IT investments.<br>▪ Formal processes for managing variances feedback into architecture definition. | ▪ Same as Level 4, with process exceptions (standards waivers) used to improve architecture governance process. |

*(continues)*

155

**Exhibit G.1    Enterprise Architecture Processes at Different Maturity Levels** *(Continued)*

| Characteristics | Level 0: No Architecture | Level 1: Initial | Level 2: Under Development | Level 3: Defined | Level 4: Managed | Level 5: Optimizing |
|---|---|---|---|---|---|---|
| **Architecture Communication** | ▪ None | ▪ There is a "notebook" documenting the last version of the architecture.<br>▪ May have been handed out to IT staff.<br>▪ New IT staff may not automatically get copies. | ▪ Notebook is updated periodically or a Web site is used to document architecture deliverables.<br>▪ Few tools (e.g., office suite, graphics packages) are used to document architecture.<br>▪ Communication about architecture process via meetings, etc., may happen, but is sporadic. | ▪ Architecture documents updated and expanded regularly.<br>▪ "Live" documentation of the architecture, via internal Web sites. Tools are used to support maintaining architecture documentation.<br>▪ Periodic presentations to IT staff on architecture process and content.<br>▪ Likely a part of new-hire training | ▪ Architecture documents regularly updated, and frequently monitored across architecture content.<br>▪ Regular presentations to IT staff on architecture process and coverage in new-hire training.<br>▪ Tracking and reporting of architecture training to IT staff (who took it, when). | ▪ Same as Level 4, with process exceptions (standards waivers) used to improve architecture communication process improvements. |

**Exhibit G.1  Enterprise Architecture Processes at Different Maturity Levels** (*Continued*)

| Characteristics | Level 0: No Architecture | Level 1: Initial | Level 2: Under Development | Level 3: Defined | Level 4: Managed | Level 5: Optimizing |
|---|---|---|---|---|---|---|
| **Program Management** | ▪ No formal project management discipline or skills exist. | ▪ Little project management discipline or skills. <br> ▪ Lack of formal priority-setting mechanism for mission plans. | ▪ Planning and scheduling activities are linked to time-based enterprise architecture developments. <br> ▪ Project risk and impact assessment conducted by the operating unit "Enterprise Architecture Working Group." | ▪ Future IT staffing requirements based on target technical architecture. <br> ▪ Change management procedures exist and linked to formal architecture review. <br> ▪ Adhere to formal project management methodology and conduct design review with the operating unit "Enterprise Architecture Working Group." | ▪ Development of program initiatives includes participation by the operating unit "Enterprise Architecture Working Group" representatives. <br> ▪ Contingency planning requirements feed into the enterprise architecture planning cycle. | ▪ Value assurance program is in effect. <br> ▪ Mission continuity planning is a core competency and plans are refreshed based on target architecture and transition planning activities. |

*(continues)*

# Exhibit G.1 Enterprise Architecture Processes at Different Maturity Levels (Continued)

| Characteristics | Level 0: No Architecture | Level 1: Initial | Level 2: Under Development | Level 3: Defined | Level 4: Managed | Level 5: Optimizing |
|---|---|---|---|---|---|---|
| **Holistic Enterprise Management** | ▪ No formal modeling techniques and documentation exists.<br>▪ No inventory of mission processes, information entities, or applications. | ▪ Mission, information, and application requirements exist only within the technical architecture. | ▪ Basic application inventory exists and is maintained.<br>▪ Business models exist as parts of the mission. | ▪ Application inventory is linked to the mission.<br>▪ Systems are classified within a basic portfolio of technical condition and mission value.<br>▪ Enterprise business models exist and are used during design and development. | ▪ Application portfolio planning and business modeling manifest within the enterprise architecture process model.<br>▪ Modeling techniques and methods are reexamined periodically to ensure content is well understood and communicated.<br>▪ Model use is measured. | ▪ Metrics gathered at Level 4 drive process improvements.<br>▪ Enterprise portfolio replaces application portfolio.<br>▪ Enterprise portfolio encompasses business logic, data, infra-structure, services, and business changes.<br>▪ Enterprise modeling is an automated competency. Models are kept current. |

**Exhibit G.1   Enterprise Architecture Processes at Different Maturity Levels** *(Continued)*

| *Characteristics* | *Level 0: No Architecture* | *Level 1: Initial* | *Level 2: Under Development* | *Level 3: Defined* | *Level 4: Managed* | *Level 5: Optimizing* |
|---|---|---|---|---|---|---|
| **IT Investment and Procurement Strategy** | ■ No strategic IT procurement strategy exists. | ■ Little or no adherence to existing standards profile.<br>■ Little or no involvement of strategic planning and procurement personnel in enterprise architecture process. | ■ Some adherence to existing standards profile.<br>■ Little or no formal governance of purchasing and order content. | ■ IT procurement strategy exists and includes compliance measures to IT enterprise architecture.<br>■ Adherence to existing standards profile.<br>■ RFQ, RFI, and RFP content is influenced by the enterprise architecture.<br>■ Acquisition personnel are actively involved in enterprise architecture governance structure. | ■ All planned IT acquisitions and purchases are guided and governed by the enterprise architecture.<br>■ RFI and RFP evaluations are integrated into the IT architecture planning activities.<br>■ Technology and application obsolescence plans are constructed and integrated into current baseline inventories. | ■ No unplanned IT procurement activity. |

# APPENDIX H

# MATURITY MODEL FOR BUSINESS ACTIVITIES IN THE EXTENDED ENTERPRISE

## MATURITY LEVEL REQUIREMENTS

In early 1970, when computer processing was implemented widely in commercial use, the general control concept over programmed procedures (system development and operation) and the application control concept for integrated manual and coverage of business process computerization were mainly for accounting and operational levels.

With the advent of Net-centric technologies, innovating the business model and business process has been the focus. The coverage of business process computerization has been expanding over even strategic/tactical planning, alliance partners' areas, and so on. In this extended enterprise environment, it is critical to establish a new control concept to cope with this new environment.

In the extended enterprise environment, there is a high risk of doing business without sufficient transparency and autonomy of business objects (encapsulation of resources and function). A certain level of maturity of information model/governance is required for enterprises initiating e-commerce with alliance/partners.

COBIT has provided a maturity model for IT Governance for evaluation of control over IT resources and activities. This test provides a Maturity Model for Enterprise Governance for evaluation of control over business resources and activities from business perspectives as follows.

# MATURITY MODEL FOR GOVERNANCE IN THE EXTENDED ENTERPRISE

## Level 0: No Existence of Information Process

There is a complete lack of any recognizable manual or computerized information process for enterprise governance. The enterprise has not even recognized there is an issue to be addressed and hence there is no communication about the issues. Only invoice level information is exchanged for settlement.

## Level 1: Initial/Ad Hoc

There is evidence that the organization has recognized that the enterprise governance issues exist and need to be addressed. There are, however, no standardized processes but instead there are ad hoc approaches applied on an individual or case-by-case basis. Management's approach is chaotic and there is only sporadic inconsistent communication on issues and approaches to address them. Each enterprise handles its own accounting information for quarterly or monthly closing. There are some batch-oriented core business systems for handling invoices. There is no standard assessment process. Enterprise governance is only implemented reactively to an incident that has caused some loss or embarrassment to the organization.

## Level 2: Repeatable but Intuitive

There is global awareness of enterprise governance issues. Enterprise governance activities and performance indicators are under development, which include core business planning, actual performance, and monitoring processes. As part of this effort, enterprise governance activities are formally established into the organization's change management process with active senior management involvement and oversight. Core enterprise processes are identified for reengineering and are effectively planned and monitored and are derived within the context of a defined business process and IT architectural framework. Enterprise resource planning (ERP) implementation normally starts along with the project initiation.

Management has identified basic enterprise governance measurements and defined governance assessment methods and techniques; however, the process has not been adopted across the enterprise. Different people undertaking the same task follow informal and intuitive procedures. Individuals drive the governance process within various reengineering projects/processes. Hence these processes are repeatable, and some of them begin to be monitored. Limited governance tools are chosen and implemented for gathering governance metrics, but may not be used to their full capacity due to a lack of expertise in their functionality. There is no formal training and communication on governance standard procedures, and responsibility is left to the individual. There is high reliance on the knowledge of individuals and therefore errors are likely. However, there is consistent communication on the overall issues and the need to address them.

## Level 3: Defined Process

The need to act with respect to enterprise governance is understood and accepted. A *baseline* set of enterprise governance indicators is developed where linkages between outcome measures and performance drives are defined, documented, and integrated into strategic and operational planning and monitoring processes. Procedures have been standardized, documented, and implemented. Management has communicated standardized procedures, and informal training is established. Performance indicators over all enterprise governance activities are being recorded and tracked, leading to enterprisewide improvements. Although measurable procedures are not sophisticated, they are the formalization of existing practices. Core ERP implementation normally has been completed and some level of integration of information is achieved. Tools are standardized using currently available techniques.

Balanced scorecard ideas are being adopted. It is, however, left to the individual to get training, to follow the standards, and to apply them. Root cause analysis is only occasionally applied. Most processes are monitored against some metrics (the baseline set), but any deviation—while mostly being acted on by individual initiative—would unlikely be detected by management. Nevertheless, overall accountability of key process performance is clear, and management is rewarded based on key performance measures.

Real time, ongoing monitoring with computer file matching control technology has been implemented and it is ready to get into e-commerce and e-business environment.

## Level 4: Managed and Measurable

There is full understanding of the enterprise governance issues at all levels, supported by formal training. There is a clear understanding of who the customer is and responsibilities are defined and monitored through service-level requirements. Responsibilities are clear and process/ business object ownership is established.

Formal strategic and tactical business planning and monitoring systems are starting to be implemented. Business processes are aligned with its mission and strategy. Improvement in business process is based primarily on a quantitative understanding and it is possible to monitor and measure compliance with procedures and process metrics. All process stakeholders are aware of risks, the importance of extended enterprise and IT, and the opportunities they can offer. Management has defined tolerances under which processes must operate. It is possible to monitor and measure compliance with procedures and process metrics and to take action where processes appear not to be working effectively or efficiently. Action is taken in many, but not all, cases. Processes are occasionally improved and enforce best internal practice. Root cause analysis is being standardized.

Continuous improvement is beginning to be addressed. There is limited, primarily tactical use of technology based on mature techniques and enforced standard tools. There is involvement of all required internal domain experts. Enterprise governance evolves into an extended enterprisewide process. IT governance activities are integrated with the enterprise governance process.

## Level 5: Optimized

There is advanced and forward-looking understanding of enterprise governance issues and solutions, leading-edge concepts/techniques, supports training, and communication.

IT is used in an extensive, integrated, and optimized manner to automate the workflow and provide tools to improve quality and effectiveness. Qualitative communication tools are widely implemented with net centric technology and knowledge base objects.

There is a clear understanding of who the customer is and responsibilities are defined and monitored through one-to-one qualitative and quantitative service level requirements. Processes have been refined to a level of external best practice, based on results of continuous improvement and maturity modeling with other organizations. The implementation of these polices has lead to an organization, people, and processes that are quick to adapt and fully support enterprise governance requirements.

Responsibilities are clear and process/business object ownership is established. Formal strategic and tactic business planning and monitoring systems have been implemented with knowledge management systems. Business tactical plans, and processes are aligned with its mission and strategy. Improvement in business tactical plan and process is based on qualitative and quantitative understanding, and it is possible to monitor and measure compliance with goal (key goal indicator, or KGI), procedure, and process (key performance indicator, or KPI) metrics. All goal and process stakeholders are aware of risks, the importance of extended enterprise, knowledge base, and IT, and the opportunities they can offer.

Management has defined tolerances under which tactical plans and processes must operate. It is possible to monitor and measure compliance with goals, procedures, and process metrics and to take action where processes appear not to be working effectively or efficiently. All problems and deviations are root cause analyzed and efficient action is expediently identified and initiated. Continuous improvement has been implemented.

Monitoring, self-assessment, and communication about governance expectations are pervasive within the enterprise, and there is optimal use of technology and best practices to support measurement, analysis, communication, and training.

The risk and returns of the IT processes and business best practices are defined, balanced, and communicated across the enterprise. External experts are leveraged and benchmarks used for guidance. Monitoring, self-assessment, and communication about governance expectations are pervasive within the organization and there is optimal use of technology and best practice to support measurement, analysis, communication, and training. Enterprise governance is strategically linked, leveraging technology and human, financial, and knowledge-based resources to increase the competitive advantage of the enterprise.

# APPENDIX I

# IT GOVERNANCE*

Enterprises rely on IT for their competitive advantage and cannot afford to apply to IT anything less than the same level of commitment they devote to financial supervision and overall enterprise governance. Increased complexity, speed, interconnectivity, and globalization mean that information technology (IT)—more than ever—can involve huge costs and enormous risks. At the same time, IT offers extraordinary opportunities to enable and transform the business. Cost, risk, and opportunity not only make IT strategic to enterprise growth, but also render it essential for enterprise survival.

Many believe that IT will be the major driver for economic wealth in the twenty-first century. Although this might be open to debate, it is clear that enterprises rely on IT for their competitive advantage and cannot afford to apply to IT anything less than the same level of commitment they devote to financial supervision and overall enterprise governance. Now is the time for boards of directors to provide necessary oversight and form dedicated IT committees.

At its core, IT governance is concerned about two responsibilities: IT must deliver value and enable the business, and IT-related risks must be mitigated. IT presents the extremes of both—very large investments and critical, potentially crippling risks. At the same time, it offers exceptional opportunities for growth and renewal.

---

*The information contained in this appendix was developed as part of the *Board Briefing on IT Governance,* 2nd edition, developed and published by the IT Governance Institute.

Governance of IT encompasses several initiatives for board members and executive management. They must be aware of the role and impact of IT on the enterprise, define constraints within which IT professionals should operate, measure performance, understand risk, and obtain assurance.

## WHY IS IT IMPORTANT TO THE ENTERPRISE?

**IT contributes directly to market value.** A key driver here is the value of information. Information and other intangible assets (e.g., human capital, brand, quality of management) are now part of the competitive agenda, and many of these assets revolve around the use of IT. Business enablement, through the use of IT, has achieved new importance in an increasingly networked marketplace. Executive management has a growing awareness of the strategic value of an organization's information assets and its ability to exploit them. As the importance of intangible assets increases, demonstrating the impact IT has on shareholder value is essential.

**IT is essential for the achievement of business goals.** Business goals cannot be achieved without IT's continuous, effective, and efficient support. This basic reality is characterized by situations such as these:

- The enterprise's inability to exist without IT, for example, airlines, banking, communications, media
- The enterprise's dependence on business models predicated on IT for supply chain management
- The inability to support revenue streams without automation
- The inability to comply with regulations or contractual service levels without IT

**IT involves large investments and business risks.** Not achieving business goals is a basic, and significant, risk of IT. In addition to sizable risks, IT involves substantial investments. These investments particularly need management's attention when they do the following:

- Are notably different from the industry average
- Represent a significant percentage of an enterprise's expense base
- Show an abnormal increasing trend
- Are as much as the enterprise's entire profits

## HOW DO ENTERPRISES PERCEIVE THE IMPORTANCE OF IT?

Surveys conducted in 2001 by Acadys (Europe) and the Standish Group (United States) found that enterprises do not treat their IT as an important enabler because the business does not treat IT as a partner or top management does not provide IT its attention, as shown in Exhibit I.1.

Furthermore, only a few are able to measure the value that IT returns above expectations, as shown in Exhibit I.2, while the majority of IT projects continue to fail, as shown in Exhibit I.3.

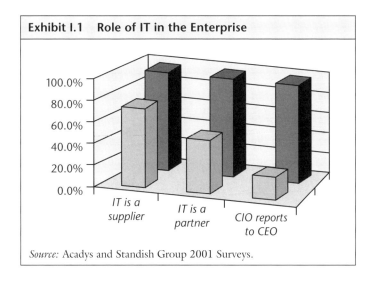

**Exhibit I.1    Role of IT in the Enterprise**

*Source:* Acadys and Standish Group 2001 Surveys.

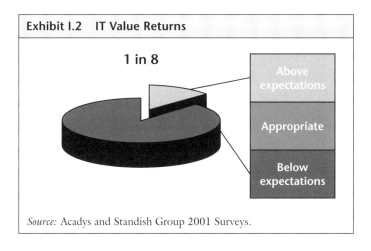

**Exhibit I.2    IT Value Returns**

*Source:* Acadys and Standish Group 2001 Surveys.

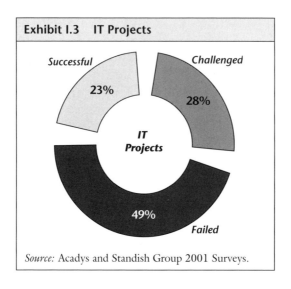

**Exhibit I.3    IT Projects**

*Successful*

*Challenged*

23%

28%

*IT Projects*

49%

*Failed*

*Source:* Acadys and Standish Group 2001 Surveys.

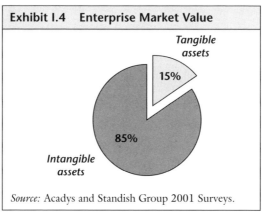

**Exhibit I.4    Enterprise Market Value**

*Tangible assets*

15%

85%

*Intangible assets*

*Source:* Acadys and Standish Group 2001 Surveys.

In addition, the actual value of information is underestimated. According to the Brookings Institute, only 15 percent of the market value of an enterprise resides in tangible assets, while 85 percent rests in intangible assets, as shown in Exhibit I.4. The largest part of those intangibles assets is information.[1]

## WHY FOCUS ON IT GOVERNANCE?

Clearly, the importance of IT must place it firmly onto the governance agenda of boards and executives. Investors have acknowledged their awareness of the importance of governance, demonstrating a willingness to pay a premium of up to 20 percent on shares of enterprises known to have a governance framework in place, as documented by a 2000 McKinsey Report. Information and its supporting technology, essential for enterprise survival and growth, have become an integral part of the governance responsibilities.

Not only are investors sending strong messages about governance, but also, society is demanding greater accountability for executives and board members in the private and public sectors. Regulators are becoming outspoken as well, addressing awareness, transparency, and accountability. For example:

- The first recommendation of the President's Commission on the Critical Information Infrastructure initiative in the United States called for awareness of corporate officers of IT risks and of the utter dependence of business on the nation's information infrastructure.
- Boards of companies listed on the London Stock Exchange must address corporate risks and be transparent about them.
- Critical systems supporting the financial industry are required by the Bank for International Settlements (BIS) to have a transparent, effective, and accountable governance structure.

Despite the extensive investments and risks inherent in IT, IT governance has not received the board attention it merits, mainly because IT oversight differs from the oversight of business strategy and risks in many ways:

- IT requires more technical insight than do other disciplines to understand how it enables the enterprise and creates risks and opportunities.
- IT has traditionally been treated as an entity separate to the business.
- IT is complex, even more so in the extended enterprise operating in a networked economy.
- IT knowledge at the board level generally has been limited.

This has meant that boards—and, to some degree, management—have been hesitant to get involved in IT governance. However, their reluctance is unfounded, because IT governance calls for sound decision making, clear process, and leadership—activities boards and management are well equipped to handle.

Sadly, past experience has not given boards a good feeling about IT. Failures, unfulfilled promises, and disappointments have been rife in all industries. Two business leaders reflect the widespread disenchantment: While he was chairman of General Electric, Jack Welch called IT the longest running disappointment in business in the last 30 years.[2] Also, Jean-Pierre Corniou, director of the department of information systems and technologies for Renault, said he was going to write a book about the history of IT—to find out why it was such a mess![3]

## WHERE DOES IT GOVERNANCE FIT?

IT governance is not a separate discipline. It is a component of enterprise governance, with the main responsibilities as follows (see Exhibit I.5):

- Taking stakeholder values into account when setting strategy
- Giving direction to the processes that implement the strategy
- Ensuring that processes provide measurable results
- Being informed about the results and challenging them
- Ensuring that the results are acted upon

IT governance involves applying the principles of enterprise governance strategically to directing and controlling IT. Specifically, it should emphasize these characteristics:

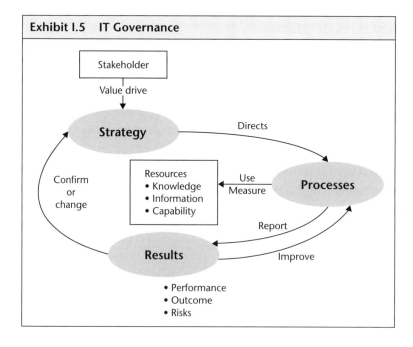

Exhibit I.5  IT Governance

- Potential of IT to leverage and influence intangible assets (information, knowledge, trust, etc.)
- Alignment of IT and business strategies
- Review and approval of IT investments
- Assurance of IT-related risk transparency
- Measurement of IT performance

IT governance is the responsibility of the board of directors. The directors exercise that responsibility by providing leadership and by ensuring IT sustains and extends the organization's strategies and objectives.

## WHAT SHOULD BOARDS DO ABOUT IT?

Board members do not need to become technology experts, but they do need to equip themselves with a high-level understanding of their changing roles and responsibilities regarding IT oversight and should consider attracting more IT-related business skills to the boardroom.

First, boards should start asking tough questions about enterprise alignment of IT, its cost, risks, opportunities, and measuring the overall effectiveness and performance. They should question whether IT is achieving its objectives and returning benefits. They should delve into its resilience in the face of increasing risks and its capitalization on the opportunities of the Information Age.

Second, boards should set up an IT strategy committee (see Exhibit I.8). Some boards hesitate to do so due to members' reluctance to sit on what may be perceived as a "technical" committee and/or the CEO's wariness at having to deal with yet another board committee. However, the importance of the IT strategy committee is such that these objections should be overcome. The committee should review and approve IT strategy, providing high-level direction and control about the value IT needs to deliver and the IT risks that need to be managed.

## WHAT SHOULD MANAGEMENT DO ABOUT IT?

The following list provides some points on how management should deal with governance issues (see Exhibit I.6):

- Management should align business and IT strategy, *cascading strategy* and goals down into the enterprise and translating them into action for employees at each level.

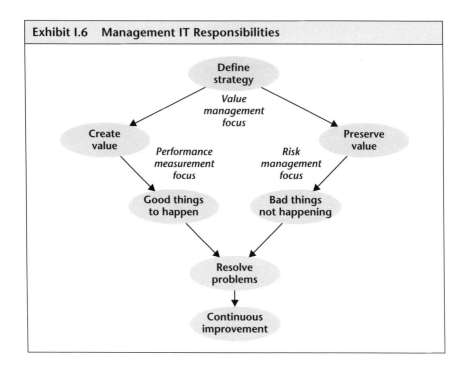

**Exhibit I.6    Management IT Responsibilities**

- After aligning business and IT strategy, management should align IT and the business organization, promoting co-responsibility for the success of IT projects and the return of *business value.*

- Management should ensure that *risk analysis* is an integral part of all planning processes, focusing on the vulnerabilities of the IT infrastructure, and the exposure of intangible assets to security and operational risks and the risk of IT project failures.

- Management should implement *performance measurement* based on the aligned strategy and goals. The emerging eminent tool for this is the *balanced business scorecard,* with the understanding that, when building an IT scorecard, the value of information defies traditional business metrics.

- Management should work to resolve problems, report on results, and use this as input to drive the continuing improvement process.

- The CIO should have the clout or influence to make these steps happen, wielding a position of authority in the organization and holding the power to say no. While currently only one in five CIOs report to the CEO,[4] that situation gradually is changing.

## HOW IS INDUSTRY MEASURING UP?

One of the major challenges for management is aligning IT with the business. There is still a long way to go. In 50 percent of the cases, IT is considered just an operator or service supplier rather than a true partner; in only 40 percent is there some form of strategy integration, and in only 20 percent is there true strategic alignment, according to a recent European survey performed by Acadys. This is confirmed by Darwin's survey in the United States revealing that in only 40 percent of the cases did IT's relationship with the business improve in 2001.

One of the major tasks for the board is to become informed and involved in IT. A survey of *Fortune* 500 companies by the IT Governance Institute in 2003 measured the responses against a scale illustrating the degree to which enterprises have begun to appreciate the importance of IT and the need to govern it (Exhibit I.7). The survey revealed that, for the private sector:

- Nine out of ten business executives recognize that IT is vital for delivering the organization's strategy

- Seven out of eight boards are at least regularly informed about IT issues

- Six out of ten boards approve IT strategy, half of them having an IT strategy committee

## HOW DOES THE FUTURE LOOK?

The predictions of reputable market analysts such as Gartner, Compass, Giga, and Computer Sciences Corporation reveal that the top issues for

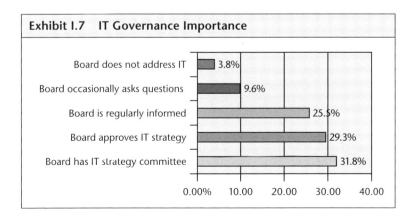

**Exhibit I.7   IT Governance Importance**

IT management in 2002 have transitioned from technology to management-related issues which clearly map to the following IT governance responsibilities:

- Strategic alignment of IT with the business
- Value delivery of IT
- Management of IT risks
- IT resource management
- Performance measurement of IT, without which the other responsibilities cannot be appropriately measured

This explains the emergence of IT balanced scorecards in more advanced enterprises. The need for IT performance management is illustrated by the same surveys referred to previously. Acadys found that only one in eight European enterprises is able to measure the value of IT. The Standish Group found that, internationally, 3 of 10 IT projects fail outright, 2 of 10 are seriously challenged and, of the remainder, more than half deliver below expectations.

## CONCLUSION

Major market analysts have shown that IT has moved from a technology issue to a management and governance issue. IT's impact on intangibles, its crucial role for survival, and the need to optimize its value make it imperative to place IT governance on the board's agenda as an integral part of enterprise governance. Good governance practices definitely affect shareholder value. The IT Governance Institute's research indicates that boards have become aware of these realities and are beginning to address the issue.

For those enterprises in which IT is a relatively small corporate expenditure, putting a governance and control framework in place for IT (see Exhibit I.8) may seem onerous. However, Dutch multinational corporation Royal Philips Electronics did not think so. With U.S. $30 billion in sales and 220,000 employees, Royal Philips spends less than 4 percent of sales on IT (it spends double that on research and development). Even at that relatively low expenditure, the board initiated an extensive enterprisewide program to assess and improve the degree of governance and control over IT processes. Why? On the one hand, margins are small so that even a 4 percent expenditure needs controlling, but, on the other hand, the board has realized the major ability of IT not just to enable, but to transform, the enterprise.

---

**Exhibit I.8   Key IT Governance Practices**

### IT Strategy Committee
The creation of an IT strategy committee is an industry best practice. However, the IT strategy committee needs to broaden its scope, not only to include advice on strategy when assisting the board in its IT governance responsibilities, but also to focus on IT value, risks, and performance. This is a mechanism for incorporating IT governance into enterprise governance. As a committee of the board, it assists the board in overseeing the enterprise's IT-related matters by ensuring that the board has the internal and external information it requires for effective IT governance decision making.

### Risk Management
Effective risk management begins with a clear understanding of the organization's appetite for risk. This focuses all risk management effort and, in an IT context, affects future investments in technology, the extent to which IT assets are protected and the level of assurance required.

Having defined risk appetite and identified risk exposure, strategies for managing risk can be set and responsibilities clarified. Dependent on the type of risk and its significance to the business, management and the board may choose to:

- *Mitigate.* For example, acquire and deploy security technology to protect the IT infrastructure.
- *Transfer.* For example, share risk with partners or transfer to insurance coverage.
- *Accept.* That is, formally acknowledge the existence of the risk and monitor it.

### IT Balanced Scorecard
Use of an IT balanced scorecard is one of the most effective means to aid the IT strategy committee and management to achieve IT and business alignment. Its objectives are to establish a vehicle for management reporting to the board, to foster consensus among key stakeholders about IT's strategic aims, to demonstrate the effectiveness and added value of IT, and to communicate IT's performance, risks, and capabilities.

# NOTES

1. The Brookings Institute, 1992, and the Lev Analysis of S&P 500 companies, 1998. This figure applies even to manufacturing companies. Trust and reputation are other increasingly important intangibles in an interconnected economy.
2. World Economic Forum, Davos (Switzerland), February 1997.
3. IT Governance Institute's IT Governance Forum, Paris (France), June 2001.
4. Independently confirmed by a Hunter Management Group survey in the United States and a European survey by Acadys (see *value.acadys.com*).

# APPENDIX J

# IT GOVERNANCE
# MATURITY MODEL*

## MATURITY MODEL FOR IT

The IT Governance Institute set up a Maturity Model for IT Governance in COBIT (3rd Edition, 2000). The benchmark survey performed in May 2002 produced interesting results, as shown in Exhibits J.1, J.2, and J.3.

The legends for the rankings used in Exhibit J.3 are further explained in the following paragraphs.

**0  Nonexistent**    There is a complete lack of any recognizable IT governance process. The organization has not even recognized that there is an issue to be addressed and hence there is no communication about the issue.

Governance, such as it is, is predominantly centralized within the IT organization, and IT budget and decisions are made centrally. Business-unit input is informal and done on a project basis. In some cases, a steering committee may be in place to help make resource decisions.

**1  Initial/Ad Hoc**    There is evidence that the organization has recognized that IT governance issues exist and need to be addressed. There

---

*The IT Governance Maturity Model was developed by the ITGI and first appeared in COBIT, 3rd ed., also published by the ITGI. This approach is based on the Capability Maturity Model Concept defined by the Software Engineering Institute for software development and capability.

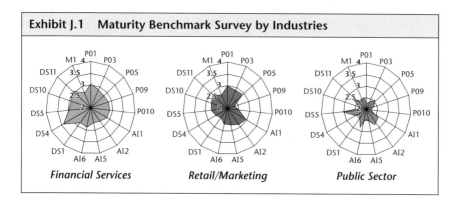

Exhibit J.1    Maturity Benchmark Survey by Industries

*Financial Services*          *Retail/Marketing*          *Public Sector*

Exhibit J.2    The Important IT Processes

| Plan and Organize | 1 | Define a strategic IT plan |
|---|---|---|
| PO | 3 | Determine the technological direction |
| PO | 5 | Manage the IT investment |
| PO | 9 | Assess risks |
| PO | 10 | Manage projects |
| **Acquire and Implement** | 1 | Identify solutions |
| AI | 2 | Acquire and maintain applications software |
| AI | 5 | Install and accredit systems |
| AI | 6 | Manage changes |
| **Deliver and Support** | 1 | Define service levels |
| DS | 4 | Ensure continuous service |
| DS | 5 | Ensure system security |
| DS | 10 | Manage problems and incidents |
| DS | 11 | Manage data |
| **Monitor and Evaluate** | 1 | Monitor the processes |

are, however, no standardized processes, but instead there are ad hoc approaches applied on a case-by-case basis. Management's approach is chaotic and there is only sporadic, inconsistent communication on issues and approaches to address them. There may be some acknowledgement of capturing the value of IT in outcome-oriented performance of related enterprise processes. There is no standard assessment process. IT monitoring is implemented only reactively to an incident that has caused some loss or embarrassment to the organization.

Governance should begin to be implemented, although a potential problem is that the central IT organization and business units may have

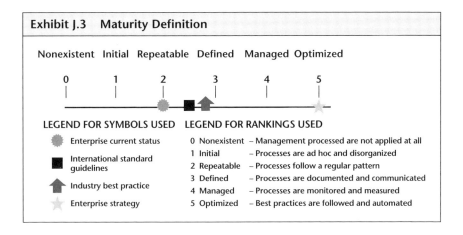

**Exhibit J.3    Maturity Definition**

Nonexistent  Initial  Repeatable  Defined  Managed  Optimized

| 0 | 1 | 2 | 3 | 4 | 5 |

LEGEND FOR SYMBOLS USED    LEGEND FOR RANKINGS USED

- Enterprise current status
- International standard guidelines
- Industry best practice
- Enterprise strategy

0 Nonexistent – Management processed are not applied at all
1 Initial – Processes are ad hoc and disorganized
2 Repeatable – Processes follow a regular pattern
3 Defined – Processes are documented and communicated
4 Managed – Processes are monitored and measured
5 Optimized – Best practices are followed and automated

an adversarial relationship. The enterprise must begin to establish the roots of an *office of enterprise IT* (if only with one or two key stakeholders) or to redirect a steering committee, if there is one. A single problem that all agree needs a solution is used to establish the beginning structure before extending the process to additional issues. Key areas of trust (and distrust) are identified to build the basis for a partnership.

**2  Repeatable but Intuitive**    There is global awareness of IT governance issues. IT governance activities and performance indicators are under development, which include IT planning, delivery, and monitoring processes. As part of this effort, IT governance activities are formally established into the organization's change management process, with active senior management involvement and oversight. Selected IT processes are identified for improving and/or controlling core enterprise processes and are effectively planned and monitored as investments and are derived within the context of a defined IT architectural framework. Management has identified basic IT governance measurements and assessment methods and techniques; however, the process has not been adopted across the organization. There is no formal training, and communication on governance standards and responsibilities is left to the individual. Individuals drive the governance processes within various IT projects and processes. Limited governance tools are chosen and implemented for gathering governance metrics, but may not be used to their full capacity due to a lack of expertise in their functionality.

The office of enterprise IT begins to formalize and establish its roles and responsibilities. There is the initial document of the core of a governance charter (e.g., participants, roles, responsibilities, delegated

powers, retained powers, shared resources and policy). Small and pilot
governance projects are initiated to see what works and what does not.
General guidelines are emerging for standards and architecture that
make sense for the enterprise and a dialogue has started to sell the reasons for their need in the enterprise.

**3 Defined Process**     The need to act with respect to IT governance is
understood and accepted. A baseline set of IT governance indicators is
developed, where linkages between outcome measures and performance
drivers are defined, documented and integrated into strategic and operational planning and monitoring processes. Procedures have been standardized, documented and implemented. Management has communicated
standardized procedures and informal training is established. Performance indicators over all IT governance activities are being recorded and
tracked, leading to enterprisewide improvements. Although measurable,
procedures are not sophisticated, but are the formalization of existing
practices. Tools are standardized, using currently available techniques.
IT balanced business scorecard ideas are being adopted by the organization. It is, however, left to the individual to get training, to follow
the standards, and to apply them. Root cause analysis is only occasionally
applied. Most processes are monitored against some (baseline) metrics,
but any deviation, while mostly being acted on by individual initiative,
would unlikely be detected by management. Nevertheless, overall accountability of key process performance is clear, and management is rewarded
based on key performance measures.
    The office of enterprise IT is formalized and operational, with de-
fined participation and responsibilities agreed to by all stakeholders.
The governance charter and policy is also formalized and documented.
The governance organization beyond the "office of enterprise IT" is
established and staffed.

**4 Managed and Measurable**     There is full understanding of IT governance issues at all levels, supported by formal training. There is a clear
understanding of who the customer is and responsibilities are defined
and monitored through service level agreements. Responsibilities are
clear and process ownership is established. IT processes are aligned with
the enterprise and with the IT strategy. Improvement in IT processes is
based primarily on a quantitative understanding and it is possible to
monitor and measure compliance with procedures and process metrics.
All process stakeholders are aware of risks, the importance of IT and the
opportunities it can offer. Management has defined tolerances under
which processes must operate. Action is taken in many, but not all cases

where processes appear not to be working effectively or efficiently. Processes are occasionally improved and best internal practices are enforced. Root cause analysis is being standardized. Continuous improvement is beginning to be addressed. There is limited, primarily tactical, use of technology, based on mature techniques and enforced standard tools. There is involvement of all required internal domain experts. IT governance evolves into an enterprisewide process. IT governance activities are becoming integrated with the enterprise governance process.

There is a fully operational governance structure that addresses a consistent architecture for re-engineering and interoperation of business processes across the enterprise, and ensures competition for enterprise resources and ongoing incremental investments in the IT infrastructure. IT is not solely an IS organizational responsibility but is shared with the business units.

**5 Optimized**   There is advanced and forward-looking understanding of IT governance issues and solutions. Training and communication is supported by leading-edge concepts and techniques. Processes have been refined to a level of external best practice, based on results of continuous improvement and maturity modeling with other organizations. The implementation of these policies has led to an organization, people, and processes that are quick to adapt and fully support IT governance requirements. All problems and deviations are root-cause analyzed- and efficient action is expediently identified and initiated. IT is used in an extensive, integrated, and optimized manner to automate the workflow and provide tools to improve quality and effectiveness. The risks and returns of the IT processes are defined, balanced and communicated across the enterprise. External experts are leveraged and benchmarks are used for guidance. Monitoring, self-assessment and communication about governance expectations are pervasive within the organization and there is optimal use of technology to support measurement, analysis, communication and training. Enterprise governance and IT governance are strategically linked, leveraging technology and human and financial resources to increase the competitive advantage of the enterprise.

The governance concept and structure forms the core of the enterprise IT governing body including provisions for amending the structure for changes in enterprise strategy, organization or new technologies.

# APPENDIX K

# CobiT INFORMATION PROCESSES

The following 34 processes are part of the CobiT Framework. A *domain* is a natural cluster of processes that usually coincides with a particular office or functional unit.

| Domain | Objective Number | Process |
|---|---|---|
| **Plan and Organize** | PO1 | Define a strategic IT plan. |
| | PO2 | Define the information architecture. |
| | PO3 | Determine technological direction. |
| | PO4 | Define the IT organization and relationships. |
| | PO5 | Manage the IT investment. |
| | PO6 | Communicate management aims and direction. |
| | PO7 | Manage human resources. |
| | PO8 | Ensure compliance with external requirements. |
| | PO9 | Assess risks. |
| | PO10 | Manage projects. |
| | PO11 | Manage quality. |
| **Acquire and Implement** | AI1 | Identify automated solutions. |
| | AI2 | Acquire and maintain application software. |

*(continues)*

185

| Domain | Objective Number | Process |
|---|---|---|
| **Acquire and Implement** (*Continued*) | AI3 | Acquire and maintain technology infrastructure. |
| | AI4 | Develop and maintain procedures. |
| | AI5 | Install and accredit systems. |
| | AI6 | Manage changes. |
| **Deliver and Support** | DS1 | Define and manage service levels. |
| | DS2 | Manage third-party services. |
| | DS3 | Manage performance and capacity. |
| | DS4 | Ensure continuous service. |
| | DS5 | Ensure systems security. |
| | DS6 | Identify and allocate costs. |
| | DS7 | Educate and train users. |
| | DS8 | Assist and advise customers. |
| | DS9 | Manage the configuration. |
| | DS10 | Manage problems and incidents. |
| | DS11 | Manage data. |
| | DS12 | Manage facilities. |
| | DS13 | Manage operations. |
| **Monitor and Evaluate** | M1 | Monitor the processes. |
| | M2 | Assess internal control adequacy. |
| | M3 | Obtain independent assurance. |
| | M4 | Provide for independent audit. |

# GLOSSARY

**Business balanced scorecard** is a tool for managing organizational strategy. It uses weighted measures for the areas of financial performance (lag) indicators, internal operations, customer measurements, learning and growth (lead) indicators combined to rate the organization.

**COBIT** (Control Objectives for Information and related Technology) was developed as a generally applicable and accepted standard for good governance information technology (IT) security and control practices to provide a reference framework for management, users, and IS audit, control, and security practitioners.

COBIT is a tool that allows managers to bridge the gap with respect to control requirements, technical issues, and business risks and communicate that level of control to stakeholders. It provides good practices across a domain and process framework and presents activities in a manageable and logical structure. The impact on IT resources is highlighted in the COBIT *Framework,* in 34 high-level process statements or control objectives where critical insight is provided to develop a clear policy and good practice for IT controls—enterprise-wide. COBIT includes the *Management Guidelines,* which are composed of maturity models, to help determine the stages and expectation levels of control and compare them against industry norms; critical success factors, to identify the most important actions for achieving control over the IT processes; key goal indicators, to define target levels of performance; and key performance indicators, to measure whether an IT control process is meeting its objective. An additional piece of COBIT is the *Audit Guidelines*.

The Third Edition was published in July 2000 by the IT Governance Institute, Rolling Meadows, IL 60008.

**Coevolving** originated as a biological term. It refers to the way two or more ecologically interdependent species become intertwined over time. As these species adapt to their environment, they also adapt to one another. Today's multibusiness companies need to take their cue from biology to survive: They should assume that links among businesses are temporary and that the number of connections—not just their content—matters. Rather than plan collaborative strategy from the top, as traditional companies do, corporate executives in coevolving companies should simply set the context and let collaboration (and competition) emerge from business units.

**Coherence** means establishing a potent binding force and sense of direction and purpose for the organization, relating different parts of the organization to each other and to the whole to act as a seemingly unique entity.

**Competencies** are the strengths of an organization, what it does well.

**Competitive advantage** is derived from understanding how to systematically create, use, and improve knowledge to make the leap from individual learning to institutional learning.

**Context** includes the factors that must be present before any specific attempt to transform enterprise systems data into knowledge and results. Includes technology context (technological factors that affect an organization's ability to extract value from data), data context (data accuracy, availability, currency, and quality), skills and knowledge (general experience and analytical, technical, and business skills), organizational and cultural context (political factors and whether the organization prefers data to intuition), and strategic context (strategic objectives of the organization).

**Critical success factors** (CSF) define the most important issues or actions for management to achieve control over and within its IT processes. They must be management-oriented implementation guidelines and must identify the most important things to do, strategically, technically, organizationally, or procedurally.

**Demographic** is a fact determined by measuring and analyzing data about a population; it relies heavily upon survey research and census data.

**Double-loop step** integrates the management of tactics (financial budgets and monthly reviews) and the management of strategy. A reporting system, based on the balanced scorecard, allows process against strategy to be monitored and corrective actions to be taken as required.

**Enterprise architecture** takes a broader view of business and information. It puts greater emphasis on business and information requirements, supports the business, and enables information sharing across different business units or so-called traditional barriers.

**Enterprise governance** is a broad and wide-ranging concept of corporate governance, covering associated organizational entities such as global strategic alliance partners.

**ERP** (enterprise resource planning) system is a packaged business software system that allows an organization to:

- Automate and integrate the majority of its business processes
- Share common data and practices across the entire enterprise
- Produce and access information in a real-time environment

**Extended enterprise** describes an organization that extends outside its traditional boundaries. Such organizations concentrate on the processes in which they do best and rely on someone outside the entity to perform the remaining processes.

**IT Governance Institute** (ITGI), founded by the Information Systems Audit and Control Association and its affiliated foundation in 1998, strives to assist enterprise leadership in ensuring long-term, sustainable enterprise success and increased stakeholder value by expanding awareness of the need for and benefits of effective IT governance. The institute develops and advances understanding of the vital link between IT and enterprise governance, and offers best-practice guidance on the management of IT-related risks.

**Key performance indicators** define measures to determine how well the IT process is performing in enabling the goal to be reached. They are lead indicators of whether a goal will likely be reached or not, and are good indicators of capabilities, practices, and skills.

**Knowledge portal** refers to the repository of a core of information and knowledge for the extended enterprise. This is generally a Web-based implementation containing a core repository of information provided for the extended enterprise to resolve any issues.

**Leadership** is the ability and process to translate vision into desired behaviors that are followed at all levels of the extended enterprise.

**Net-centric technologies** such as the Internet view the network as its primary concern. The contents and security of information or objects (software and data) on the network are now of prime importance compared with traditional computer processing that emphasizes the location of hardware and its related software and data.

**Organization for Economic Cooperation and Development (OECD)** is an international organization helping governments tackle the economic, social, and governance challenges of a globalized economy. The OECD groups 30 member countries in a unique forum to discuss, develop, and refine economic and social policies.

**Patching** is bridging between new initiatives to achieve holistic results. It is referred to as the frequent remapping of business to fit changing market opportunities.

**Performance indicators** define measures to determine how well the IT process is performing in enabling the goal to be reached; are lead indicators of whether a goal will likely be reached or not; and are good indicators of capabilities, practices, and skills.

**Strategic planning** is the process of deciding on the organization's objectives, on changes in these objectives, and the policies to govern their acquisition and use.

**SWOT** (strengths, weaknesses, opportunities, and threats) is a combination of an organizational audit listing the organization's strengths and weaknesses and an environmental scan or analysis of external opportunities and threats.

# REFERENCES

Bacheldor, Beth. "Amazon.com Aims to Provide Everything to Everyone." *Information Week,* vol. 5, no. 2 (May 22, 2000), pp. 26.

*Board Briefing on IT Governance,* 2nd edition. Rolling Meadows, IL: IT Governance Institute, October 2003.

Cadbury Report is the common name for the report by the committee on the Financial Aspects of Corporate Governance set up in May 1991 by the U.K. Financial Reporting Council, the London Stock Exchange, and the U.K. Accountancy profession, chaired by Sir Adrian Cadbury.

Collins, Jim. "Level 5 Leaderships: The Triumph of Humility and Fierce Resolve." *Harvard Business Review* (January 2001).

CobiT (Control Objectives for Information and related Technology) *Framework.* Rolling Meadows, IL: IT Governance Institute, 2000, *www. isaca. org/cobit.*

*Control Objectives Net Centric Technology, Intranet/Extranet/Internet.* Rolling Meadows, IL: Information Systems Audit and Control Association, 1999.

*Criteria for Performance Excellence.* Baldrige Quality Program, U.S. Department of Commerce, 2002.

*Criteria of Control.* Canadian Institute of Chartered Accountants, 1995.

Cuisumano, Michael A., and C. Markides Constantinos, editors. *Strategic Thinking for the Next Economy.* Massachusetts Institute of Technology/San Francisco: Jossey-Bass, 2001.

Curran, Thomas, Gerhard Keller, and Andrew Ladd. *SAP R/3 Business Blueprint.* Englewood Cliffs, NJ: Prentice Hall, 1998.

Davenport, Thomas H. *Mission Critical.* Boston: Harvard Business School Press, 2000.

Dallas, Susan. "CIO Update: IT Governance Rules to Boost IS Organization and Business Unit Credibility." Gartner Research, December 4, 2002. *www4. gartner.com/displaydocument.*

Dell, Michael, and Catherine Fredman. *Direct From DELL.* New York: Harper-Collins, 1999.

Deming Prize. *www.deming.org/demingprize/prizeinfo.html.*

Drucker, Peter. *The Information Executives Truly Need.* Boston: Harvard Business School Press, 1998.

Drucker, Peter. "The Discipline of Innovation." *The Harvard Business Review* (November–December 1998).

Dyche, Jill. *E-Data, Turning Data into Information with Data Warehousing.* Reading, MA: Addison Wesley, 2000.

Eccles, Robert G. *The Performance Measurement Manifesto.* Boston: Harvard Business School Press, 1998.

Eisenhardt, Katheleen M., and Shonal L. Brown. "Patching: Restitching Business Portfolios in Dynamic Markets." *The Harvard Business Review* (May–June 1999).

Eisenhardt, Katheleen M., and D. Charles Galunic. "Coevolving: At Last, a Way to Make Synergies Work." *The Harvard Business Review* (January–February 2000).

*Enhancing Corporate Governance in Banking Organizations.* Bank for International Settlements, 1999.

Enterprise Architecture Development Tool-Kit V2.0, Adaptive Enterprise Architecture Development Program, National Association of State Chief Information Officers (NASCIO), Lexington, KY, July 2002.

"Fifth Annual Special Report on Technology in Banking—Creating the Value Network." Financial Services Consulting Practice, Ernst & Young LLP, Boston, MA, 1996.

Federal Enterprise Architecture Framework Version 1.1. The Chief Information Security Council, September 1999.

Finkelstein, Clive. "Enterprise Architecture for Senior Managers." *The Enterprise Newsletter* (October 2000).

Flohr, Thomas. "IT: Know Thyself." *Intelligent Enterprise,* vol. 5, no. 15 (May 15, 2000), pp. 59–62.

Garvey, Martin J. "Dell: Beyond the Box." *InformationWeek,* vol. 5, no. 22 (May 22, 2000), pp. 49–59.

Garvin, David. *Learning in Action.* Boston: Harvard Business School Press, 2000.

Ghosh, Anup K. *E-Commerce Security, Weak Links, Best Defenses.* Hoboken, NJ: John Wiley & Sons, 1998.

Goleman, Daniel. "Leadership that Gets Results." *Harvard Business Review* (March–April 2000).

*A Guide to Project Management Body of Knowledge* (PMBOK guide) defines project management as the application of knowledge, skills, tools, and techniques to project activities to meet project requirements. Project management is accomplished through the use of processes such as initiating, planning, executing, controlling, and closing. Project Management Institute, Philadelphia, PA, 2002.

Gustin, Craig M., Patricia J. Daugherty, and Theodore P. Stank. "The Effects of Information Availability on Logistics Integration." *Journal of Business Logistics,* vol. 16, no. 1 (1995), pp. 1–21.

Hammer, Michael. *Beyond Reengineering*. New York: HarperCollins, 1996.

Handfield, Robert B., and Ernst L. Nichols, Jr. *Introduction to Supply Chain Management*. Englewood Cliffs, NJ: Prentice Hall, 1999.

Hansen, Morten T., Nitin Nohria, and Thomas Tierney. "What Is Your Strategy for Managing Knowledge?" *Harvard Business Review on Organizational Learning*. Boston: Harvard Business School Publishing Press, 2001.

Hock, Dee. *Birth of the Chaordic Age*. San Francisco: Berrett-Koehler Publishing, 1999.

Ikujiro, Nonaka. "The Knowledge-Creating Company." *Harvard Business Review on Knowledge Management*. Boston: Harvard Business School Press, 1998.

Information Technology Management Reform Act. "Clinger-Cohen Act," United States, enacted January 1996.

*IT Governance Summary.* Rolling Meadows, IL: IT Governance Institute, 2002.

Kaplan, Robert S., and David P. Norton. "The Balanced Scorecard—Measures that Drive Performance." *The Harvard Business Review* (January–February 1992).

Kaplan, Robert S., and David P. Norton. *The Balanced Scorecard*. Boston: Harvard Business School Press, 1996.

Kaplan, Robert S., and David P. Norton. "Double-Loop Management: Making Strategy a Continuous Process." *Balanced Scorecard Report*. Boston: Harvard Business School Press, 2000.

Kaplan, Robert S., and David P. Norton. *The Strategy-Focused Organization*. Boston: Harvard Business School Press, 2001.

Kelly, Kevin. *New Rules for the New Economy*. New York: The Penguin Group, 1998.

Kim, W.C., and R. Mauborgne. "On the Inside Track." *Financial Times* (April 7, 1997), p. 10.

The King Report on Corporate Governance for South Africa, 2001.

Kirn, Steve. "The Balanced Scorecard at Sears: A Compelling Place for Feedback and Learning." *Harvard Business Review*, vol. 2, no. 4 (July–August 2000).

Korper, Steffano, and Juanita Ellis. *The E-Commerce Book Building the E-Empire*. San Diego: Academic Press, 2000.

Lainhart, John W., IV. "Why IT Governance Is a Top Management Issue." *The Journal of Corporate Accounting & Finance,* vol. 12, issue 5 (2000).

Lopez, Jorge. *Strategy of Acceleration: Time to Change Culture and Architecture.* Gartner Research, July 29, 2002, *www.gartnerg2.com/research/rpt.*

Mack, Robert, and Ned Frey. "Six Building Blocks for Creating Real IT Strategies." R-17-3607, Gartner Group, December 11, 2002.

Mather, H. "Design for Logistics: The Next Challenge for Designers." *Production and Inventory Control,* vol. 25 (Fourth Quarter 1992), pp. 7–10.

Matsuda, Takehiko. "Enhancing Organizational Intelligence Thought: Effective Information System Management." *The EDP Auditor Journal* (EDP Auditors Foundation, Carol Stream, IL), vol. 4 (1988).

Morin, Therese, Ken Devansky, Card Little, and Craig Petrun. *Information Leadership: A Government Executive's Guide.* NY: PricewaterhouseCoopers, LLP, 1999.

Narayandas, D. "Dell Computer Corporation." Boston: Harvard Business School Marketing Case, October 1995, revised September 1996.

Ostroff, Frank. *The Horizontal Organization.* New York: Oxford University Press, 1999.

Pande, Per S., Robert P. Neuman, and Roland R. Cavanagh. *Six-Sigma Way: How GE, Motorola, and Other Top Companies Are Honing Their Performance.* New York, NY: McGraw-Hill, 2000.

Pasternack, A. Bruce., and Albert J. Viscio. *The Centerless Corporation.* New York: Fireside, 1998.

Price Waterhouse LLP. *CFO-Architect of the Corporate's Future.* Hoboken, NJ: John Wiley & Sons, 1997.

Pottruck, David S., and Terry Pearce. *Click and Mortar.* San Francisco: Jossey-Bass, 2000.

Randolf, Alan. "Real Empowerment? Manage the Boundaries." *The Harvard Business Review,* vol. 2, no. 4 (2000).

Rigdon, W. Bradford. "Information Management Directions: The Integration Challenge." Chapter 7, in *Architecture and Standards,* 1989. Gaithersburg, MD: National Institute of Standards and Technology (NCST), Information Systems Engineering Division, National Technical Information Service, U.S. Department of Commerce.

Rosen, Evan. "Videos with Value." *InformationWeek* (October 4, 1999), pp. 112–121.

Siegel, David. *Futurize Your Enterprise-Business Strategy in the Age of the E-Customer.* Hoboken, NJ: John Wiley & Sons, 1999.

Slouka, Mark. *War of the Worlds: Cyberspace and the High-Tech Assault on Reality.* New York: Basic Books, 1995.

Sweat, Jeff. "Learning Curve: Enterprise Resource Planning Software." *InformationWeek* (August 2, 1999).

Tapscott, Don, Alex Lowey, and David Ticoll. *Blue Print to the Digital Economy*. New York: McGraw-Hill, 1998.

Vinet, R. "Business–to–Business: E. Commerce to Lead the Way." *E. Commerce Today*, vol. 96.11.29 (1996).

Wallace, Bob, and Robin Gareiss. "No Letup in Demand for E-Services." *Information Week* (January 10, 2000), p. 115.

# OTHER ITGI PUBLICATIONS

All publications come with detailed assessment questionnaires and work programs. For further information, please visit *www.isaca.org/bookstore* or e-mail *bookstore@isaca.org*.

### CoBiT® 3rd Edition

*Control Objectives for Information and Related Technology* (CoBiT) incorporates generally applicable and accepted international standards for good practice of IT management and control. It applies to enterprisewide information systems, including personal computers, minicomputers, mainframes, and client-server environments. CoBiT is based on the philosophy that IT resources need to be managed by a set of naturally grouped processes to provide the information an organization needs to achieve its objectives. To ensure the delivery of pertinent and reliable data, CoBiT provides a framework of IT control objectives that can be implemented and monitored within enterprises.

The Third Edition of CoBiT enhances the existing framework by including management guidelines, which provide additional concepts and tools for managing IT processes. Key goal indicators, critical success factors, and key performance indicators are provided for all of CoBiT's high-level control objectives. In addition, maturity models have been developed to support the planning and monitoring of the evolving IT capabilities. The Third Edition also expands concepts of IT governance and has been updated to reflect new and revised international references. A new update is expected in late 2005.

### IT Governance Implementation Guide

The guide provides readers with a methodology for implementing and improving IT governance using CoBiT. The guide focuses on a generic methodology for implementing IT governance, covering the following subjects:

- Why IT governance is important and why organizations should implement it
- The IT governance life cycle
- The CoBiT framework

- How CoBiT is linked to IT governance and how CoBiT enables the implementation of IT governance
- Stakeholders who have an interest in IT governance
- A road map for implementing IT governance using CoBiT

### IT Control Objectives for Sarbanes-Oxley

The publication explains, step-by-step in a road map approach, the current focus on enhancing corporate accountability, the audit committee's responsibility, the need to adopt and use an internal control framework (COSO), the need to consider fraud in an audit or review of internal control, the necessary but unique challenge of focusing on IT controls and using a compatible IT governance framework (CoBiT), and how to seize the opportunity of turning compliance into a competitive challenge. The document provides IT professionals and organizations with assessment ideas and approaches, IT control objectives mapped into COSO for disclosure and financial reporting purposes, and a clear road map to deal with the murkiness of these regulatory times.

### CoBiT Security Baseline

CoBiT covers security in addition to all the other risks that can occur with the use of IT. Using the CoBiT framework, this guide focuses on the specific risks of IT security in a way that is simple to follow and implement for all users—small to medium enterprises, executives and board members of larger organizations, as well as home users. It is available through the ISACA Bookstore at *www.isaca.org/bookstore.*

### Control Practices

*Control Practices* extends the capabilities of the CoBiT framework with an additional level of detail. The CoBiT IT processes, business requirements, and control objectives define *what* needs to be done to implement an effective control structure. The creation of control practices provides the more detailed *how and why* needed by management, service providers, end users, and control professionals, helping them to justify and design the specific controls needed to address IT project and operational risks and improve IT performance.

### CoBiT Mapping: ISO/IEC17799:2000 to CoBiT

The first deliverable was a global overview of the most important standards relative to control and security of IT and how they relate to each other on a high level. The second deliverable is a detailed mapping of ISO17799 to *Control Objectives for Information and related Technology* (CoBiT).

### CoBiT Mapping: Overview of International IT Guidance

The first deliverable is a global overview of the most important standards relative to control and security of IT and how they relate to each other on a high level. The second deliverable is a detailed mapping of BS7799 (ISO17799) to

*Control Objectives for Information and related Technology* (COBIT). The research includes:

- An overview of the most important standards relative to control and security of IT
- A demonstration of the possible integration of COBIT with other standards into live IT processes
- A high-level overview of COBIT, COSO, ITIL, BS7799/ISO 17799, ISO 13335, ANSI, TickIT, and the Common Criteria—ISO 15408

### COBIT Quickstart

COBIT *Quickstart* is based on a selection of COBIT's control objectives from the majority of COBIT's IT processes, together with the major critical success factors and the most important metrics that can be used to monitor performance and the achievement of goals. *Quickstart* provides a baseline for control over IT in small to medium enterprises (SMEs) and other entities where IT is less strategic and not as critical for survival.

### Control Objectives for Net-Centric Technology (CONCT)

While advances in network computing technology have given users greater access to information resources, they have also created the need for global best practices in the cyberspace environment. This four-volume set contains a framework and volumes on intranet/extranet/Internet, online transaction processing, and the data warehouse, each containing audit steps, control guidelines, and suggestions.

# INDEX